Apologetics and Evangelism

J. V. LANGMEAD CASSERLEY

D1500556

THE WESTMINSTER PRESS

Philadelphia

PRINTED IN THE UNITED STATES OF AMERICA

For
CHARLES UPCHURCH HARRIS
with respect and affection

Contents

A Note on Westminster Studies
in Christian Communication

These Studies are predicated on the ground that the Christian faith needs to be made relevant to persons in the modern world in terms of the dynamic nature of the faith itself and the channels that are capable of conveying such a faith. In itself any technique of communication conceivably could serve as well for secular as for religious ends. In this series a wide variety of means and methods of communication will be analyzed in the light of their availability to, and suitability for, the particular tasks that the Christian church faces in bringing the realities of faith to bear upon the life of actual persons in the contemporary situation.

Oftentimes in the past, techniques have been viewed almost as ends in themselves. Or, they have been taken over uncritically from the secular culture without being subjected to adequate scrutiny as to whether they are appropriate for the church's use. On the other hand, sometimes the church has been blind to the life situations of the present to such an extent as to ignore the real ways in which people's lives are influenced by all that impinges on them. In the latter case, the church has failed to bring the life-giving power of the gospel to bear on contemporary culture because of a lack of understanding of, or appreciation for, the means of communication that have been proved capable of changing lives and societies.

Involving as it does both the "What" and the "How," the whole question of the communication of the gospel in the modern world is pivotal in the present juncture of history. The present Studies will be aimed at bringing the "What" and the "How" together fruitfully. These books are designed to make a contribution to the ongoing conversations across boundaries. Theology, Biblical studies, sociology, cultural anthropology, psychology, education, art, letters, science, and the other disciplines all have something to say to one another. In our present concern, "communication" refers to the way in which the Christian faith can come into conjunction with what is happening in the total world of life and ideas in the middle decades of the twentieth century. In each of these Studies attention will focus on some important aspect of the basic question: How can the church most effectively preach, teach, and otherwise manifest the gospel in the growing edges of man's present-day culture? No aspect of man's actual situation is alien to such a question. No medium of communication should fail to come under scrutiny if, as Christians, we are eager to have the Word of God confront a confused generation powerfully and compellingly.

Each volume in Westminster Studies in Christian Communication will be an authentic voice of one perceptive interpreter. No effort has been made to suggest to any writer what "line" he ought to follow. Each work will be adjudged by the readers on its own merits. The writers themselves conceivably might disagree heartily with regard to certain presuppositions or conclusions held by their colleagues. All this will be to the good if the result of these Studies should be the stimulating of many conversations. Yet all the writers have in mind a focus that is realistic, an emphasis that is practical, and a discussion that is timely. The only request made of the authors is that they speak out of their knowledge to the very heart and mind of our times. Depth without dullness, breadth without diffuseness, challenge without sentimentality — these, at least, it is hoped, will be characteristics of all the Studies. We are grateful to those who have consented to share in this venture into communication, and we commend their work as in itself an integral part of the church's task of communication.

KENDIG BRUBAKER CULLY
General Editor

Evanston, Illinois

Preface

The basic plan of this book is one that is very simple to outline. First of all, the writer must clearly state his problem and then proceed to locate it in its proper context. After that he must critically discuss some of the proposed solutions of the problem which are widely prevalent and entertained in his own day, giving what seem to him to be the appropriate reasons for doubting whether in fact these proposed solutions have any lasting value. Finally he must state and defend his own proposed solution. The problem that is discussed in this book is that of the widespread suspicion and lack of understanding between those in the Christian church whose task it is to conduct an evangelistic, pastoral ministry among the mass of the members of the church, and those who exist upon its fringes, and those called apologists, whose function is to conduct the intellectual statement and defense of Christian truth.

The context of this problem is a sociological one: the wide gap that exists in this or any other society between the intellectual elites and the great mass of the people. Inevitably, this book is very much taken up with the criticism of points of view that the author regards as misconceived in theory and undesirable in practice; and it concludes with a brief statement and defense of his own point of view, which, to his mind, possesses the great advantage of being not merely his own but also that which is embraced in the central and enduring intellectual traditions of Christianity. The author's own academic training and background were first of all in sociology, secondly in philosophy, and thirdly in theology. So, perhaps inevitably, he occupies a position on the frontiers of these three subjects, particularly at that point at which they most closely approach one another. Hence, the book is in part a sociological one, in part a philosophical one, and in part theological. It is very much concerned, in other words, with the mutual relevance of the sociological, the philosophical, and the theological disciplines.

It must certainly always be the case that the theologian cannot hope to be very much of a theologian unless he is also a philosopher. This is widely recognized, although perhaps doubted by those for whom theology is primarily a matter of history and the literary interpretation of the Bible. What is perhaps less often realized is that neither the philosophical theologian nor the theologically inspired philosopher can operate without a wide degree of sociological understanding and insight. For in the long run, both theology and philosophy must stand or fall by the effectiveness with which they succeed in evolving intellectual and religious formulas, capable of guiding and inspiring the life and experience of the great masses of mankind. Hence, the real aim of the philosophical and theological discussions in this book is to assist and counsel the clergy and others who are busily engaged moving to and fro in the life of the church, attempting to present, to proclaim, and to teach the Christian gospel in such a manner as to stimulate and generate authentic Christian spirituality in the lives of those large numbers of ordinary men and women who fall within the orbit of their influence.

J. V. L. C.

Chapter I

The Masses and the Elites

In modern democratic societies the distinction between the masses and the elites corresponds very roughly to that between the plebs and the patricians in earlier societies. True, the hereditary element looms less large. The boundary between mass and elite is less clearly defined and more easily crossed than that between plebeian and patrician. We are more conscious of individual worth nowadays, and pedigree counts for less. However, heredity presumably still counts for something. Other things being equal it is probable that more elite children will be born into the families of elites than into the families of the masses. Environment or social heredity also accounts for a great deal. The family life of the elites is more stimulating than the family life of the masses, and hence will more effectively foster and intensify the natural gifts of those who are raised and trained within its sphere of influence. Thus in the modern democratic society hereditary forces will count for rather more in practice than they are supposed to do in theory. But undoubtedly a certain number of the children born to the masses will join the elites, and conversely a certain number of those born to the elites will find their true home within the mass life around them.

The chief characteristic of the masses is a kind of general capacity for life. The typical mass man is not a dramatically gifted individual, but he has a certain aptitude for negotiating the crises and transitions of ordinary existence which we dignify with some such title as "common sense" or "general intelligence."

Characteristic of the elites, on the other hand, are peculiar skills or abilities that have been fortunate enough to receive a high degree of training and development. Thus the elites are more diversified than the masses. We may distinguish between industrial and commercial elites, political elites, aesthetic elites, literary elites, scientific elites, intellectual elites, and so on. Not only may we validly distinguish between these distinct types of elite, we may also observe that the elites themselves distinguish one another in these ways and attach peculiar importance to doing so. Thus members of an aesthetic elite may take a very low view of the political or the commercial elite and vice versa.

If we have no class system, then it becomes necessary to invent one. The gap between the indiscriminate concept of the human race, mankind in general, and the highly abstract concept of the mere individual is too great to be endured in itself. It needs to be supported and reinforced by a large number of intermediate groupings, which break up the mass concept of the human race into nations, classes, vocations, families, and so on, thus producing groups small enough for the individual to breathe in, environments so light that the weight of them can be borne by the fragile person. Otherwise, individuality is either suffocated by the heavy weight of society or reduced to a vain irrelevance if it endeavors to stand apart from society and to be simply itself alone.

Now, it is not the purpose of this book to pursue any general inquiry of a sociological kind into the nature, social characteristics, and functions of masses and elites in contemporary society. We shall be concerned with this important sociological distinction in only one peculiar connection: its influence and effect upon the forms of Christian propaganda, the modes of the church's communication with the world. Thus we shall be concerned with the characteristics of masses and elites only in so far as these characteristics are relevant to an inquiry into the nature, content, and manner of Christian propaganda. In examining a subject like Christian propaganda, or the church's communication with the world, our point of view may be either descriptive and factual — in which case we shall try to give an account of it as it is in existing circumstances — or normative — in which case we must endeavor to see a vision of it as it could and should be if it were completely true to its proper vocation and purpose. In this book we shall use both points of view: the descriptive standpoint in order to detect and diagnose a grave danger to the church's intellectual integrity and honesty of purpose, and the normative point of view in order to catch a vision of the tremendous opportunity that confronts Christian intellectualism. It is also the case that once we have wrestled with the problem of the relationship between elite experience and mass experience, elite thought and mass thought, as it confronts us within Christianity, we may discover that in the course of our investigation we have observed and delineated certain basic principles capable of a wider employment that may enrich our sociological understanding in general as well as our Christian self-understanding in particular. So that at last a book whose main purpose is to serve the church may well discover that, without intending to do anything of the kind, it has also served the world.

Certainly we cannot possibly discuss the relationship between the refined and sophisticated, elite theological thought that we find in the heart of the church and the more general religious life of the great mass of Christian people in entire detachment from that relationship between elite intellectualism and the popular mass culture that surrounds it which is characteristic of any society. Clearly, for example, there is an analogy between the relationship of Plato to the general Athenian culture of his time and that of Thomas Aquinas to thirteenth-century Christianity, or, to select a contemporary example, that of Paul Tillich to contemporary American Protestantism.

The vocation of refined, critical, and constructive thought to its primary environment, out of which it comes and to which it addresses itself, is fundamentally similar in each of these three cases. The vocation of Christian thought and expression in relationship to its primary context and environment is identical with that of all conscious intellectualism in its relationship to popular culture. No doubt Christian thought ought to be more vividly aware of the intellectual vocation, more subtly and pervasively influenced by its proper motives, than elsewhere, but basically the relationship between conscious intellectualism and popular culture is the same everywhere. The role of conscious intellectualism is always one of service and leadership, service without idolatry, leadership without debasing compromise. Its characteristic motives must always be loyalty and love. The consecrated elite will serve the mass culture and the mass life loyally because it knows that this mass life is its inevitable and proper context. The elite life can arise within the mass life, but the mass life could never arise from within the elite life. Our choice is not between a totally mass life or a totally elite life but rather between a mass life unserved and unguided by the elites, either because it lacks them or because it ignores them, and a mass life to which the elite life makes its full and proper contribution. The idea of a pure elite life, without any kind of popular or mass environment, is as inconceivable as the idea of a fish without water.

Again, the elite must learn to serve and lead the mass with love because it knows that masses consist of persons just as truly as elites consist of persons. If there is a danger that masses should despise and ignore elites, there is an equal danger that elites should turn from the mass life with contempt and seek an introverted, sophisticated existence in which they live for themselves alone. Only with loyalty and love, therefore, can the elites perform their function and fulfill their vocation to serve and lead. And this principle is as true in the nation and the secular society as it is in the church. Certainly it will be the basic principle that will guide and control the contents of this book.

Now it is often said, and, as it seems to me, with a measure

of undeniable truth, that in contemporary society the gap between the masses and the elites is perhaps wider than ever before. The great mass of our fellow citizens cannot understand
our contemporary science — they can learn to use it technolog-
ically but without any comprehension of the processes they employ. They do not read the best contemporary literature, or, if
they do, only because its vendors have encouraged them to
think it salacious, and not in the least for the reasons that persuade our professors of literature to acclaim, for example, *Lady
Chatterley's Lover* as an important book by one of the greatest
of modern novelists. Similarly, they do not for the most part
enjoy modern art, comprehend contemporary philosophy, or
listen with delight to the music of twentieth-century composers.

In this situation the intellectuals too often react by dismiss-
ing the masses as too stupid to understand them and retiring
into a clique life of their own, in which their gifts and achievements are discreetly exhibited for the admiration of their peers.
Once, for example, we had people's poets, and even Shake-
speare tickled the ears of the groundlings. Later we had poets'
poets, and now at last we have the critics' poets, whose verses
are more likely to be praised in the pages of the discerning
literary quarterly than to be read with pleasure in the homes
of the people. Similarly with music, science, philosophy, and
even theology. Nowadays it takes an expert to understand another expert, to appreciate his skill and evaluate his achievement, and such men are well satisfied by the polite applause
of their equals.

So far as we can tell, earlier class systems often had a greater
cultural solidarity and the masses had a warmer appreciation
and deeper understanding of what the elites were doing. The
aristocrat of an earlier age, whether excelling in military or
agricultural leadership, at least performed services that the
mass could understand and value. Nowadays it is far easier to
cross the barrier that divides the masses from the elites, and
the barriers are, in fact, far more frequently crossed, yet at the
same time the distance has become far wider. The crossing is

easier and more frequent, yet paradoxically more hazardous and costly. There is at least something to be said for the view that our contemporary, democratic version of the class system is the worst version of all, breeding a distaste for the masses in the sophisticated elite and a contempt for the elite in a brutalized mass. The masses dismiss intellectualism as irrelevant, while the elites identify the intellectual superiority and spiritual beauty of their objectives and pursuits with a presumed mental superiority inherent in themselves, which renders them the cultural and moral superiors of the kind of life and personality which surrounds them.

We have to ask ourselves the question: How far is all this true within the church? The Christian church has its intellectual elites, its theologians and scholars, often tempted in the same way to perform their functions merely for the admiration of their peers, often tempted also to despise the popular religion and simple piety going on around them, as an inferior manifestation of spirituality with which they can have little or no intercourse and to which they find it almost impossible to address themselves. More and more they tend to represent an elite Christianity that estranges itself from popular Christianity, not altogether without a certain pharisaical self-satisfaction. The result is that Christian propaganda itself tends to be split between two increasingly detached forms of activity.

There is, first of all, a primarily evangelistic and pastoral *popular* ministry that addresses itself to the masses. At its very worst it simply panders to the egotisms, inferiority complexes, and anxieties of the masses in a fashion that reduces Christianity to a series of semispiritual, semipsychological recipes for brave and successful living, or to a preoccupation with the theme of religious or faith healing. But, at its best, it takes the form of a strong reaffirmation of the Biblical witness to the act of the living God in Christ, given with a passionate sincerity by latter-day witnesses whose testimony has within it a quality of manifest zeal and almost supernatural integrity, which makes a profound impression on the minds and spirits of those who receive it, thus gradually taking them out of the world's point of view and into the church's point of view, and producing phenomena like conversion, sanctification, and the spiritual or devout way of ordering and directing the personal life.

Side by side with this, however, we find in the church another kind of ministry which we may call the apologetic ministry. It is, above all, the ministry of the Christian elites to the non-Christian elites, with whom these Christian elites have often more in common socially and psychologically than with the great majority of their coreligionists.

Clearly we shall have to subject both these ministries to a much more precise and critical analysis than is possible or desirable in what is, after all, only the introductory chapter to the whole book. For the moment, let us merely note the consequences of a growing misunderstanding between these two, in themselves equally valid, types of ministry, and of the mutual suspicions that disturb their relationship. The fact of the matter is that to an increasing extent the evangelists feel themselves betrayed by the apologists, to such an extent indeed that we are confronted with the danger of a deliberately untheological or even antitheological manifestation of Christianity. On the other hand, the apologists often feel themselves embarrassed by the manifestations of religious life and conviction characteristic of the mass life of their churches and tend to retreat into an elite Christianity that in fact is incapable of either evoking or sustaining any mass church life at all. It is a Christianity of acceptable Christian ideas rather than one based on the saving acts of God; a philosophical alternative to, rather than the intellectual complement of, the real Christianity of the great majority of ordinary Christian people.

Nor is this lack of sympathy and understanding between the elite apologists and the popular evangelists by any means the whole of the trouble. Since the church itself supports and provides both the evangelistic ministry to the masses and the apologetic ministry to the elites, its own intellectual integrity is in no little danger if it discovers that these two ministries, each strengthened with its own sanction, are really saying, in effect, not merely distinct but sometimes irreconcilable things. Thus the evangelist will still strongly affirm the miraculous episodes in the gospel, for example, the virgin birth and the empty tomb, for the evangelist's aim is to shock and startle people out of one point of view into another. The apologist, on the other hand, is often tempted to seek out some sophisticated technique by means of which he can explain such episodes away. For his aim is not to shock his own particular audience out of one point of view into another but rather to persuade it that Christianity can be seen and affirmed from its own existing point of view, so that his task is to add Christianity on to what it knows and understands already rather than to supplant one way of understanding with another. The consequence for a church that sponsors both types of ministry may very well be a genuine loss of intellectual integrity and an increasingly bewildered feeling within it that really it knows not where it stands.

It is important in discussing this gap between the masses and the elites, both in the church and in the world, to avoid the mere taking of sides. Neither the mass mind nor the elite mind is entirely to blame for the estrangement, and no doubt both must accept a measure of guilt. The difficulty is that the kind of book which observes the fact of this chronic estrangement, and attempts some analysis of it, is inevitably a contribution from the intellectually elite side written by the kind of person who finds it easier to sympathize with the elites than with the masses, easier to discern their characteristic virtues and contributions. Thus in the literature and discussion of such a subject the standpoint of the masses tends to go unobserved; or, perhaps worse, in the writings of what we may call the left-wing elites, to be rather crudely patronized with elitish gestures of respect for the proletarian point of view which remind us of the ancient flattery of some inferior king by a group of professional courtiers.

In fact both the elite and the mass points of view are corruptible and often corrupted. The corruption of the elite point of view is to be found in its prevalent sophistication, a rootless use of intellectual skill to set forward merely personal points of view in conscious contradiction of derided intellectual positions which are either natural to man universally, or at least natural to man in the culture in which this sophistication occurs.

The term "sophistication" emerges out of the educational work and thought of the ancient Sophists. Sophistic thought has two primary characteristics. In the first place, it is merely critical thought. Of course, all rational thought is critical, and in particular all rational thought should aim at being self-critical. Merely critical thought, however, is not notably self-critical. The peculiar target of its criticism is not itself but what we may term mass thought (without attempting for the moment any careful analysis of what this phrase connotes) and its characteristic products, the historical, cultural, and social forms in which the life of the mass of the people is embodied and expressed. Its attempt is to substitute a self-consciously rational culture and society, rooted merely in the cerebrations of elites, for the actually existing, historically rooted forms of culture in society. Thus its tendency is to produce forms of culture and society of, by, and for the elites in which the masses cannot feel at home. The second, and consequent, characteristic of sophistication is that it takes the form of an ideology, in the Marxist sense, which cloaks and facilitates the social and cultural ambitions of the elites, for inevitably the culture and society of, by, and for the elites must be one in which the elites are the masters.

Ideally the elites are the servants of a culture that they have not made, and could not have made, but of which they are the interpreters and defenders. Thus the elites are essential to the preservation of the purity and integrity even of the historic societies and cultures that they have not made. The trouble comes when the elites are no longer content to serve the society and culture that they have not made, merely by understanding it and diagnosing and expounding its true character, but rather desire to be masters in a culture and society that they themselves have made. Thus in ancient Greece the underlying aim of the Sophists, whether acknowledged or not, was to overthrow the historic foundations of the Greek city-state and to replace it with some ambitious construction of their own. Sophistication is thus the characteristic vice of the elite.

Another aspect of elite sophistication may be more clearly diagnosed and defined in Freudian rather than in Marxist terms. Elite dissatisfaction with mass life and thought contains an element of what we may call chronic dissidence. Often the elites, with some objective justification, feel that their gifts and services are undervalued by the society in which they function, and this frequently evokes in them an understandable, if hardly a justifiable, resentment against those who seem to pass them by on the other side. Sophistication must also be understood as a rationalization of this resentment, and of the feelings of inferiority that accompany it. The tragic consequence of these corrupt elements in elite thought and motivation is a chronic frustration of intellectualism. In such a psychological atmosphere the intellectual cannot function and fulfill his vocation with integrity, and mass society itself is deprived of his services and is infinitely the poorer for such a deprivation.

Mass thought (and here again we earmark the term for later analysis, because mass thought is certainly not thought in the ordinary sense of the word) also has its characteristic perversion, which we may term brutalization. By brutalization we refer to an exaggeration of the characteristic concreteness of mass thought into some form of materialism. By materialism in this context we do not refer, of course, to metaphysical materialism (i.e., some specific form of the doctrine that matter in motion is the only reality). This doctrine, after all, is an elite performance, an attempt to re-establish the unity of masses and elites at the lowest possible level by means of an elite, sophisticated intellectualization of mass thought in its brutalized form. The materialism to which we refer is rather an ethical and economic materialism, the assumption that the only things worth striving for or bothering about are physical satisfactions, that the only social activities which in the long run really matter are economic activities. Ethical materialism puts a high value on physical comfort and on physical activities accompanied by a pleasant feeling tone, like sex; economic materialism is particularly concerned with the activities that produce wealth and express the condition of being wealthy, with acquisition, expenditure, and consumption.

Thus we are confronted with three possible relationships between elite thought and mass thought: (a) A self-sufficient mode of elite thought, sophistication in the purest sense of the word, which completely ignores mass thought in either its authentic or its brutalized form. (b) A form of elite thought for which mass thought at its broadest and best is a primary datum. The main task of elite thought in this case is to understand and express the virtues of mass thought, with a view to rendering culture and society sufficiently conscious of them to be able to defend and preserve them. (c) A sophisticated form of elite thought which reunites itself to mass thought by providing an intellectual expression of its brutalized forms.

We are going to argue in this book not only that of these three alternative relationships between elite and mass thought (b) is incomparably the best but that, in past philosophy, the primary, underlying purpose of the truly great thinkers has been such a relationship between mass thought and elite thought as our formula (b) envisages. Further, we want to argue that it is as true in the church as in the world that mass thought and elite thought cannot be drawn together merely by an education of the masses which gradually transforms them into elites. Rather, each must approximate gradually toward the other: the masses in the direction of the elites through education, the elites in the direction of the masses by a truly humble willingness to understand the strength and virtues of mass thought, and an ability to give such strength and virtues the characteristically conscious, intellectual, and critical, elite modes of expression.

Truly healthy cultural forms contrive to hold together both mass thought and elite thought and to unite them by continually approximating each to the other. Elite thinking in contempt of mass thought produces mere ideology and the characteristic *hubris* of the dogmatic rationalist, who is critical of everything except himself. Mass thought, on the other hand, without the guidance of elite thought wanders blindly through the pathways of history, unable to understand even its own excellence and in continual danger of degenerating into merely brutalized and corrupted forms.

The worst danger of all, however, is that these brutalized and corrupted forms of mass thought should provide the primary datum and inspiration of new reductionist forms of elite thought, recalling the sophistical enemies of Plato, or the *minute philosophers* and philosophies so brilliantly satirized and attacked by Bishop Berkeley. But in this chapter we have gone as far as we can go with our terms "elite thought" and "mass thought," contrasting and relating them, as we have tried to do, in various ways, so long as the terms themselves remain unanalyzed and unexplained. We can proceed no farther until we have subjected each of them in turn to minute and careful analysis. It is with this analysis that we must now occupy ourselves.

Chapter II

The Treason of the Intellectuals

The title of this chapter is obviously indebted to M. Jules Benda's justly celebrated book *La trahison des clercs*. But I am not conscious that the book itself has exercised very much influence upon what I shall have to say in this chapter, apart, that is, from a general realization that there really has been a treason of the intellectuals in the modern world, so that the blame for the estrangement between elite thought and mass thought cannot entirely be laid at the door of the latter.

We have already diagnosed two alternative forms of intellectual treason: (*a*) a dogmatic, sophisticated rationalism that contemptuously ignores mass thought altogether and (*b*) a sophisticated but subservient, indeed sycophantic, intellectualism that gives pseudointellectual expression to mass thought in its more degraded and brutalized forms. The first of these forms of treason may be described as right-wing rationalistic idealism. Sociologically it is particularly associated with the social and cultural predominance of the middle classes in the advanced Western countries during the nineteenth century, when it was especially characteristic of their cultured elites. In the twentieth century it still survives, minus the rationalism, of course, in some fashionable forms of existentialist thought. The second, alternative form of the treason of the intellectuals may be described as left-wing rationalistic materialism. It received confident and dogmatic expression in Marxism but is to be found also in other forms of economic materialism, in a great deal of modern positivism, and perhaps also in metaphysically materialist and sensationalist and ethically physicalist forms of existentialism, such as that characteristic of Jean-Paul Sartre. The former departs from the central purpose and vocation of authentic intellectualism by striving to ignore mass thought altogether, the second by flattering and paying court to mass thought only in its degraded and corrupted forms. It is probably true to say that an enormous proportion of contemporary intellectualism is treasonable in either the one way or the other.

Within the church we may say that the dogmatic right-wing intellectualism is the paramount influence in the development of the various liberal and modernist theologies and versions of Christianity which have exercised such enormous influence in Christendom during the nineteenth and twentieth centuries. Something analogous to the left-wing forms of intellectual deviation is to be found today in the revival of a sophisticated, elitish fundamentalism such as finds expression in America in the pages of that highly sophisticated and often brilliant journal *Christianity Today,* which has as its main task to take popular sect Christianity at its worst and to give pseudointellectual expression to its characteristic points of view. We can understand this sympathetically enough when we interpret it as a theological reaction against the modernistic and liberal theologians of a former age, but we cannot refrain from pointing out that it is in its own way equally treasonable.

· However, we cannot intelligibly discuss this concept of intellectual treason without clearly discerning and defining precisely what it is that has been betrayed. In order to understand the true office of authentic intellectualism we must now consider the cultural and social functions actually performed by the truly great philosophers in our Western tradition. We must begin somewhere, and I propose to select Plato as my principal illustration of authentic Western intellectualism in its best and most responsible mood.

The social and cultural phenomenon by which Plato was confronted was the decline of the city-state, a complex of institutions, customs, and achievements rooted in history and by Plato's day falling into an increasingly grave time of troubles. Certainly in the Socratic dialogues Plato appears to resemble a brilliantly gifted Sophist, despite the fact that the ordinary Sophists were so often the target of his satire and invective. The Sophists were "merely" critical of the customs and institutions of the city-state. They were indeed its internal enemies. While the enemies without gathered round its walls with the object of overthrowing its visible achievements, the Sophists were busy undermining its foundations from within.

The city-state was, of course, particularly vulnerable against the attacks of the Sophists precisely because it was a product of mass thought or, as we might say, of history. Now it is characteristic of mass thought that it has no thinkers, for mass thought is essentially the thought that no one thinks. Its intellectual structure is the structure of history, the structure that underlies the coherence of events. No one thinks mass thought; it is merely there, and unfolds its consequences and implications not in the mind of some mass thinker but in the actual history of the social and cultural forms that emerge out of the mass life. Mass thought is never speculatively conscious of itself and is therefore incapable of undertaking its own defense. That is why at times of crisis it requires the service of what we may call the dedicated elite thinker, the elite thinker for whom the structures and achievements of mass thought are a primary datum, whose task it is to make these implicit structures explicit, and thus, by defining them and comprehending their implications and presuppositions, to express them in an intellectually defensible form.

As we see authentic elite thought magnificently embodied and expressed in Plato we observe that this is precisely what he does. In the *Republic*, for example, he begins with the history of the city-state as an essential preliminary to perceiving and defining its excellence. For the city-state and its social virtues and values are for Plato the great product of the inarticulate mass thought. But now that this mighty consequence of inarticulate historical-intellectual development is challenged, it can be defended only if it can be understood and defined. The task of the elite thinker, as we find it fulfilled in Plato, is thus to understand and define the excellence of mass thought and to express it in intellectually defensible form. What was once prescribed by nature, he seems to say, must now be imposed by art,[1] for this is always the way of true social development. Thus the great work of his ideal " philosopher king " is not to set up a new social order but to reconstitute and preserve an old and " natural " one. In history the great things happen first of all without forethought or deliberate design, at all events without the forethought or deliberate design of man. It is only at a later stage that it is possible for men to understand what has happened, to appreciate the splendor of the achievement, and so to defend and maintain it.

Of course this transition from what is merely designed by nature to what must now be imposed by conscious art is far wider and more universal than the particular dilemma of the Greek city-state. For example, in the twentieth century we have been confronted by a similar transition in the all-important matter of the reproduction of our own species. In earlier times men reproduced their own kind merely by " doing what comes naturally," to quote from that excellent musical *Annie Get Your Gun*. Now, however, we have reached a period in human history in which this is no longer necessarily the case. Now the question of whether and to what extent to reproduce our own kind is becoming more and more a matter of conscious forethought and deliberation. Now we have to understand what it was that nature was doing for us in the centuries during which we gave very little thought to the matter, and to will to do what was once done for us by our own unpremeditated adhesion to nature's purposes. Again what was once prescribed by nature must now be imposed by art. The purpose of this transition, let it be noted, is not to replace the old instinctive society with an entirely new, conscious and rational, planned society but rather to continue the old instinctive society on the new basis of conscious will. Plato, in the *Republic*, is not advocating a new society but rather the carrying on of the old society on a new basis.

In this sense we may describe Plato as the true conservative, who sees that cultural and social life is indeed full of things well worthy of conservation but that at this juncture in history they can no longer be conserved in the old way. Let the new arts impose precisely what the old nature prescribed. Thus the ancient philosophy of Plato is much more like modern science than would at first sight appear. He is concerned to observe, diagnose, and define an intellectual structure already implicit in the order of events. He is certainly not concerned with thinking out for himself, by a possibly crude, possibly brilliant, act of improvisation, an entirely new intellectual structure with which to supplant the existing structure.

From this point of view Plato's *Republic* is very like a later and in some ways inferior, although almost equally famous, book, Edmund Burke's *Reflections on the French Revolution*. For Burke also, the intellectual structure is in the event before it is in the mind, and he has the same suspicion of intellectual structures that are in the mind before they are brutally imposed on the events. For him also, the first work of the mind is to understand and appreciate the magnificence of what has happened already, and then to proceed to consider under what conditions events of the same quality are likely to continue to occur. So understood, Burke's *Reflections on the French Revolution* is in the great Platonic and Western tradition. A book often opposed to Burke's, Tom Paine's *The Age of Reason*, is by comparison an inferior sophisticated product. Tom Paine, we may say, worked himself up into such a pitch of rational frenzy about dead birds that he quite forgot to admire the magnificence of their plumage. This grave error of taste was not only antiaesthetic, it was also antihistorical and anti-intellectual. Paine was blind to the greatness of history, in a way that Burke and Plato most certainly were not.

To say this, of course, is by no means to support merely conservative attitudes in politics. The strength of the conservative mind is its awareness that history has brought forth achievements worthy of conservation. Its weakness is its chronic tendency to locate these achievements in the wrong place, and to dedicate itself to a series of doomed attempts to conserve the unconservable. Perhaps even Plato was not altogether immune from this weakness. Certainly Burke was not. Yet, even while noting their mistakes, it is still possible to say that they employed the right method. They were both men who appreciated the nature and achievements of mass thought and dedicated their own elite thinking to the task of explicating and defending it.

This insistence that the intellectual structure is in the event, or better, in the course of events, before it is in the mind — which we find in both Plato and Burke — is also basic to the Anglo-Saxon empiricism in philosophy; and, of course, to Christian theology, with its stress on revelation, on a series of events embodying and revealing an intellectual structure in terms of which the eternal relationships of God and man must be comprehended. Indeed empiricism in Anglo-Saxon philosophy and revelationism in theology have a great deal in common with each other. For both it is not sufficient merely that the intellectual structure should be plausible enough to convince the reason. It must not only convince the reason but also dominate the event; or, rather, it cannot properly convince the reason unless it also dominates the event. Rationality for the empirical mind is never pure rationality but rather rationality plus actuality. For many modern radical minds Burke has threatened this principle by giving it a subtle twist which makes it the basis of a conservative political philosophy. But that is merely one aspect of its much wider and more comprehensive validity. In any case, even the politically radical mind will prefer a conservatism that is Burkeian and intelligent to a conservatism that is merely crass and undiscriminating. If we want to appraise the quality of the conservative mind, we must first of all find out precisely what it is that it proposes to conserve. If it is trying to conserve everything in general, then we may dismiss its conservatism as mere undiscriminating prejudice. If, however, it is trying to conserve the positive achievements of the past, distinguished from merely ephemeral elements in the past by an act of intellectual analysis, then the political radical must recognize that he is dealing with an intelligent man in every way as rational and conscientious as himself.

Our formulation of the Burkeian principle: Let the intellectual structure be in the event before it is in the mind, and not vice versa, certainly clashes in some ways with the well-known Marxist dictum: It is not the function of thought to reflect reality but to change it. On the other hand, the normally dominant Hegelian element in Marxist thought does not entirely fit in with this assertion. Marx, after all, is satisfied that his basic intellectual structure is indeed both embodied and revealed in the course of past events. In his view, however, this basic intellectual structure when properly understood is a dialectical process that implies the necessity of a future event that has not yet occurred. There are, of course, analogies to this in the Christian philosophy of history. For Marx, history up to now makes no sense without some reference to the future worldwide communist revolution and the coming of the classless society. For Christian thought, history up to now makes no sense without some reference to the coming of the Kingdom of God.

Both Marxism and Christianity thus adopt a thoroughly eschatological view of history, even though they differ radically about the nature and character of the *eschaton* itself. For both, however, the intellectual structure that demands that we infer the necessity of the *eschaton* is already revealed in the events that either have taken place or are taking place. Thus both conform to our general rule that the intellectual structure must be first in the events and only subsequently in the mind, rather than the other way about. For both it is the events that reveal and the mind that understands what is thus revealed.

The main difference between Marxism and Christianity, on the one hand, and Burkeian conservatism, on the other, is that for the latter the intellectual structure embodied and revealed in the events is a closed and completed structure; whereas for the former it is a dialectical process that is sufficiently revealed in the events for us to be able to detect the character of its implications, and yet nevertheless not totally revealed. For all three the notion that a pure, virgin rationalism may improvise or excogitate out of itself a rational pattern that can subsequently be imposed on events in some sort of planned, elite society is anathema. The purely rationalistic planned society would necessitate a dictatorship of the rationalistic elites, and it is against this that all the instincts of mass thought and culture tend to revolt.

So far Plato and Burke have been our principal illustrations of our view that it is the function of elite thought to grasp the virtues of mass thought comprehensively and to give them an articulate expression of which mass thought is of itself quite incapable. Now perhaps, in order to make a transition from philosophical to theological thought, we may select two other examples of a similar intellectual process: the Genesis story of the Fall in the Garden of Eden and the medieval natural law theory of legislation and the state.

In the Genesis story Adam and Eve are presented to us as the primitive and primordial parents of the human race, living in a luxuriant fertile jungle in a state of almost animal innocence. They are naked food gatherers and their way of life is precisely that which we must attribute to the very first human beings. Resembling the higher primates to a remarkable degree, they pick berries from bushes, fruit from trees, and dig edible roots from the earth. Their fall is their primitive failure to make the leap from innocence to righteousness at the point at which such a step was necessitated by the process of their evolution. In a way innocence and righteousness are remarkably alike; in another sense there is a decided difference between them. Innocence is enjoyed instinctively without forethought or deliberate will; righteousness, on the other hand, must be consciously willed and intended. Apart from this im-

portant distinction the actual content of innocence and righteousness is identical. They differ not in the content but in the
mode of their being. To become truly human, to rise to the
fullness of the new human stature, a transition from innocence
to righteousness is absolutely essential. It was the failure to
make this leap with success that we call the fall, a falling short
of the indicated and necessary objective.

It was through the fall that all subsequent social and human
structures became corrupted ones, fallen well below the level
of their potentialities. Man had indeed become man but not
totally — not with entire success. He had become man without
achieving the stature indicated by the richness of the human
potentiality. Nevertheless, when we have said that innocence
is the proper subject matter of righteousness, or, conversely,
that righteousness is innocence transposed and repitched into
the appropriate human key, we have illustrated once more our
general theme that the structure in the mind must always be
the structure that was previously indicated and given in the
event, that as human development takes place there is a continual taking over of unconscious and instinctive material by
the understanding, and a rewilling of it by the self-conscious
person. The intellectual pattern is precisely the same as that
which we have traced in Plato and Burke. Let the intellectual
structure first be perceived in and disentangled from the actual
texture of the event, and then let it be vigorously affirmed and
willed by the conscious mind.

We find this same intellectual pattern in the medieval theory
of the state and the law. According to this view, the state is not
the legislator or lawgiver. Rather, the state observes and recognizes the law from its own study and analysis of the existing
and previous social structure and then enforces and applies it.
In the medieval view, God the Creator is the only lawgiver,
and the law was given with and in the creation itself. According to this view, there are three possible approaches to a
knowledge of the law which converge upon and reinforce one
another. All three can be found side by side in medieval

writers. One is through the actual study of the word of God;
i.e., of a Biblical document such as the Ten Commandments.
To this we may add an analytic study of actual social structures, leading us to a consideration of the norms and shapes
which they spontaneously display and of the basic conditions
of social health and well-being implied by what we observe
when we examine them. The third way is a consideration of
actual social processes, for in a sinful world the so-called natural law of God for man is to be observed as much by its absence, and by the catastrophic consequences of its absence, as
by its presence and the ensuing blessings that it brings with it.
In history, whether history as interpreted by Hebrew prophets,
or by Greek philosophers like Plato, or by a Christian philosopher-theologian like Augustine, we detect the will of God, or
the law of human historical and social nature, primarily by ob-
serving the consequences of our disobedience to it, and the extraordinary fascination that it exercises over us and the pull
toward it which historical societies experience even when they
have denied and almost forgotten it.

Thus what we know through the revelation of the Ten Commandments could conceivably be known even apart from and
without the Ten Commandments by an empirical and analytical
survey of actual social forms and forces. It is interesting to note
that there is indeed in Christian theology a point of view from
which it can be affirmed that a secular basis for morality is
possible. It is often supposed in anti-Christian and rationalist
arguments that the belief that a secular basis for morals exists
is the very antithesis of Christianity, whereas, in fact, we find
such a belief enshrined in traditional catholic orthodoxy. What
the theologian doubts is not so much the possibility of a speculative knowledge of moral law apart from Christianity and the
grace of God, but rather the actual existence of a historical and
social tradition in conformity with the moral law apart from
Christianity and the grace of God. This kind of skepticism is,
after all, a necessary ingredient in the theologian's make-up,
and it is precisely because the modern world has been imbued

with so much faith in the potentialities of mere history, and in the capacity of secular social and political processes to bring forth the redeeming values, that the theologian so often seems to be present in the modern world primarily as a destructive skeptic, as a dissident type of mind, spreading gloom and defeatism among the common people.

Thus, according to this kind of social philosophy, the laws that prescribe and describe the actual conditions of healthy human association and development are identical with the laws of God. The task of the legislators is not to make the law but to discover and recognize the law and so both to affirm it and to apply it to the changing conditions that arise in the course of history. In a way this medieval philosophy of the state and of legislation remarkably resembles modern sociology. For what is modern sociology but an empirical survey and analysis of the actual forms of human coexistence and society, with the object of discovering laws that describe them, and of articulating norms of social health and excellence by means of which the further progress and development of society can be fostered and facilitated? Both in medieval social philosophy and in modern sociology we find the same insistence that the intellectual structure is immanent in the event that the mind contemplates before it becomes conscious and explicit in the mind itself.

But the thought of the medieval theological elites illustrates our general theme in wider and profounder fashion than this. We may select as a further example by far the best known today, if not perhaps the greatest, of the medieval philosopher-theologians, Thomas Aquinas. The particular form of sophistication with which Thomas Aquinas was confronted was the theory of the double truth, popular in the faculty of arts in the thirteenth-century University of Paris, and particularly associated with the name of Siger of Brabant. According to this theory, what was true in the order of philosophy, identified with the writings of Aristotle as interpreted by Averroes, usually called Latin Averroism, need not be true in theology, and what was true in theology, identified with the Biblical revela-

tion, need not be true in philosophy.[2] We shall see later that
other versions of this double truth theory are still with us, and
indeed it remains one of the characteristic forms of elite sophistication.

Aquinas set his face firmly against any such sophistication.
For him all truth is God's truth, and even though the reason of
man might for the moment be incapable of envisaging all truth
as one single rational system, it is certainly the case that the
reason of God does just that, and that the reason of man must
therefore try to follow humbly in the footsteps of the divine
reason. Therefore accepting, as a man of the thirteenth century, the general view of the time that the writings of Aristotle
were a compendium of natural truth (i.e., of philosophical and
scientific truth), Aquinas attempted in a series of great systematic writings to show that this truth was at all points compatible, not merely with a new elite version of Christianity provided by himself, but with the general, authentic Christianity
of the great mass of Christians. If his task as a philosopher was
to understand the intellectual structures explicit in Aristotle,
his task as a theologian was to comprehend the intellectual
structures implicit in the faith, life, and worship characteristic
of the historic Christian church and, without opposing the one
to the other, to reveal the two as composing a single coherent
system of thought.

It is not the function of the Christian philosopher-theologian
to frustrate the church or to confuse its faith, nor is it the function of the Christian theologian to frustrate or deny the claims
of science and the intellect. The greatness of Aquinas is to be
found in his faithfulness to the life and actuality of the living
church on the one hand and to the claims of the intellect on the
other. He represents the intellectual church making manifest
its integrity, and for this reason he is the patron saint and hero
of theologians imbued with a similar ideal to this very day.
One does not need to be a Thomist in order to hymn the praises
of Thomas. In the thirteenth-century situation Aristotle and
Averroes represent the elites, whereas the general Christianity

of the Catholic Church represents the masses. Thomas represents the elite mind, achieving not merely a mastery of its own
proper elite material but also a sympathetic understanding of
the implicit mass thought underlying the whole structure of
the mass life. In this sense Thomas' relation to the medieval
church, gravely threatened by Manichaean heresy and the rising vogue of classical paganism, is identical with Plato's relation to the Greek city-state. Thomas came not to change it but
rather to perpetuate by understanding it, to strengthen its will
to survive by helping it to achieve self-consciousness, and thus
to become itself more vigorously in a season of crisis and
change.

From this point of view the function of elite thought is not
so much to show the masses where they are wrong so that they
may become something other than what they are, but rather to
teach them where they are right so that they may will to be
what they already are with greater effectiveness and integrity.
One is reminded of what is perhaps the essence of Sören
Kierkegaard's existentialism: first, discover who you are and
then will to be what you are with greater effectiveness, because
now you clearly know and deliberately will in the light of day
what before you inherited without knowledge and carried on
impulsively and instinctively in the dark. The analogy with the
procedures of much modern psychoanalysis is also plain and
striking.

When we come to the Reformation we have moved away
from this high constructive point of view. Now, the function of
elite theological thought is to show the church where it has
been wrong rather than to help it to understand where it has
been right so that it may continue to be right with greater integrity than in the past. No doubt it is true that the great Reformers really and sincerely desired to reform the church, but
the fact of the matter is that they had not sufficient understanding of the characteristic excellencies of the church's traditions
to succeed in such a venture. Here and there, for example, in
the Church of England and the later Anglicanism which grew

out of the English Reformation, and perhaps, to a lesser extent, in the Church of Sweden, they did succeed in achieving a genuine re-formation of the church. But for the most part what came out of their work was the establishment of relatively large new Christian sects and not a genuine re-formation of the existing church at all. As reformers of the church they failed; it was as innovators of new religious institutions they succeeded, thus bequeathing to contemporary Christendom a problem that it now tries desperately and somewhat clumsily to solve.

Indeed we can trace in the Reformation all the characteristic vices of elite thought. The Reformers were theological elites, estranged from the mass life that was their proper context, and giving their estrangement and dissidence a theological rationalization. At the same time their thought contained an ideological element, because, after all, the Reformers became the first leaders and architects of the new kinds of religious society which emerged from their agitations. The enthronement of the revolutionaries is always the first and primary achievement of any revolution, a consideration that should make us healthily skeptical of all revolutionary movements. Thus, to sum up this phase of the discussion, the proper office of elite thought is to understand the implicit wisdom and achievement of mass thought, to restate it explicitly, to integrate it with the cultural achievements and enrichments that only elite thought can provide, and to exhibit the whole in a systematic intellectual structure that will frustrate neither the masses nor the elites but rather exhibit them as twin aspects of a single growing and dynamic human culture.

Characteristic therefore of elite thought at its best is its empiricism, its historicism, its revelationism. By empiricism here I mean of course more than the merely physical, sensationalist empiricism of the eighteenth-century Anglo-Saxon epistemologists, with their rather dreary preoccupation with sense data. In their view the only thing that we can know for certain is the continuous, ever-changing stream of sense data, and their problem was how, out of our acquaintance with sense data, to derive any knowledge of the real world. To this problem there seemed to be only two possible conclusions: (1) that we cannot know reality as it is in itself, and must therefore remain skeptical about any kind of reality distinct from or running deeper than the mere stream of sense data, and (2) that the kind of reality manifested by sense data is the only kind of reality there is, so that apart from sense data there is no reality to be known. This latter conclusion seems to cut us off from any possible knowledge of the divine reality. But if it made it impossible for us in any sense to understand or recognize God, it also raised another problem, for it made it impossible for us in any sense to understand or to recognize ourselves. Somehow the human reality as well as the divine reality must necessarily escape the grasp of such a philosophy as this.

The alternative affirmation to this sensationalistic empiricism is to say that what confronts us in experience and what we know in knowledge are not sense data at all. We do not know sense data, rather *we know by means of sense data,* so that what is genuinely known in knowledge is some aspect of reality that reveals itself in and through sense data, while at the same time in its own being transcending sense data. This introduces us to a very different kind of empiricism, according to which all experience is revelation of that which lies beyond it, but no possible human experience completely comprehends that which reveals itself in all experience. Reality is certainly immanent in experience, but with equal certainty it transcends it, so that philosophically we must say of reality what theologians say of God; i.e., that he is both transcendent and immanent at the same time.

This is sometimes supposed to be a paradox, but it may be doubted whether this is really the case. Transcendence and immanence are a pair of metaphysical terms that necessitate and imply each other, so that there can be no transcendence without immanence and no immanence without transcendence. Abstract transcendence without immanence is no more than mere otherness, and not really transcendence at all. Abstract immanence without transcendence is no more than mere identity, and not really immanence at all. The term "immanence" is meaningless unless it means the immanence of the transcendent. Similarly the term "transcendence" is meaningless unless it means the transcendence of the immanent. God, if we are theologians, or reality, if we are philosophers, is neither wholly other nor completely identical. He is revealed because he is immanent. He needs to be revealed because he is transcendent. Thus empiricism in philosophy and revelationism in religion can be shown by such an analysis to amount to very much the same thing. But, of course, the empiricism that recognizes this has passed far beyond the mere sensationalistic empiricism whose end product is the natural sciences as they stood at about the close of the eighteenth century. This broader empiricism must learn to be empirical not merely with regard to nature but also with regard to cultural history and the depths and subtleties of human existence. It is thus through a primarily historical empiricism that the elite thinkers can arrive at their understanding of the wisdom and achievement of inarticulate mass thought.

Here again we must note that by historicism we mean not primarily the devotion of the mind to mere historical research in the narrow sense of the word. Rather, we mean a preoccupation with historical and social experience that produces some comprehension of what issues are at stake in historical and social existence and conflict. The problem for the historian is not merely the problem of what happened in history; it is also the problem of what history is about, what is at stake in history. For history embodies not merely changing events but also abiding purposes and what we may call chronic themes, occurring and recurring in all history with invincible persistence, and with an endless profusion of subtle disguises, which the genuine historian of man and of human culture must learn to unmask. Thus it is, once more, that by revelationism I do not mean mere bibliolatry or fundamentalism but rather an understanding that in the Biblical events there are specifically disclosed the patterns of relationship between God and man in terms of which man must achieve his self-understanding before God, and in terms of which he is led to regard his understanding of God as both logically and historically prior to any possible understanding of himself. " It is the God-relationship," said Kierkegaard, " which makes a man a man." Thus some understanding of God is inevitably prior to any understanding of ourselves.

The main drift of this discussion is toward the view that the essence of elite thought in general, with its all-pervasive empiricism, and Christian thought in particular, with its sharpened and specialized Biblical empiricism, is to be found in the particular kind of historicism in which they converge. If the rule of thought is that the intellectual pattern is to be found implicit in the event before it can become explicit in the mind, then a certain radical seriousness about the event must be one of the primary characteristics of elite thought. On the other hand, one of the most tragic failings of rationalistic thought, in the bad sense of the word " rationalistic," has been its tendency to be much more interested in ideas than in events, so that it tends again and again to obvert the necessary relationship between idea and event. Thus, according to what we may term the left-wing elite mind — we refer here to the middle-class radical rationalist, not the Marxist — the idea must first of all be conceived and born in the mind of the elite thinker, and then subsequently imposed as an alien pattern upon an otherwise anarchic course of events. Even when, as in some elite Christian thinkers, it is conceded that the event may have played some part in the original revelation and birth of the idea, it may still be held that once the elite thinker has ruthlessly squeezed the idea out of the event it may then be held and defended as pure, self-authenticating idea, and the event itself cast aside as though it were of no further value.

It is here that we come to a new consideration of the way in which so many of the Christian elite thinkers of the nineteenth and twentieth centuries have betrayed the Christian masses, and the church of which the masses are inevitably the chief constituent, by constantly seeking in one way or another to transform Christianity into a matter of pure, self-authenticating ideas, and to conceal, deny, or brush aside its basic dependence upon the Biblical testimonies to historical events.

The phase in the development of Christian thought which we are now about to describe belongs primarily to the history of Protestantism, although it has not been altogether without effect upon and within Catholicism. Nevertheless, it is within the Protestant tradition that it arises, and we have to consider what those elements were in classical Protestant theology which helped to make it possible. First, however, we must character-ize in the broadest possible terms the complex and many-sided movement that we have described as the treason of the Chris-tian intellectuals. We may say that the most significant charac-teristic of the many and diverse theological movements that are usually described as either "modernist" or "liberal," both terms being very loosely used, is a certain relative indifference to the sheer actuality of Biblical events. The motives for this in-difference, and the theological use that is made of it, vary sig-nificantly, however, the variation stemming from the very na-ture of theology.

Theology as a form of reason, or as a way of applying and using reason, falls somewhere midway between history and philosophy. There have been theologians who were little more than historians, historians either of Biblical events or of the development of Christian theological thought. In the modern world a primarily Biblical-historical approach to theology has been encouraged in many countries because it makes it easier for universities to provide interdenominational theological de-partments. The result is that many contemporary theologians have been trained in the Biblical-historical approach to the-ology and have come to regard it as the normal form of theo-logical studies. The great classical Christian theologians, how-ever, leaned more heavily in the philosophical direction. People

like Athanasius, Augustine, and Aquinas were theologically inspired philosophers and certainly not historians in any sense at
all. Thus within the field of theological studies we find historians who are not philosophers and philosophers who are in no
sense historians and, of course, many intermediate blended
types. Theology itself, however, is the reconciliation or synthesis of philosophy and history, which is one reason, perhaps,
why theologians often find themselves particularly interested in
the problems of the so-called philosophy of history. Thus we
must distinguish between theologians who are really Christian
philosophers, and theologians who are little more than Biblical or ecclesiastical historians.

When we find both types of theologian sharing this general
indifference to the sheer actuality of the Biblical events, they
will be doing so for very different reasons and probably with
very different theological consequences. The historian-theo-
logian will tend to dismiss the actuality of Biblical events because research and speculation have convinced him that the
available evidence is insufficient to enable him to assert their
actuality with any degree of confidence and integrity. This type
of theologian tends to attempt a reconstruction of a reduced
Christianity based simply upon a theological interpretation of
those Biblical events which in his view we are warranted in affirming with confidence and integrity. For this kind of reduced
Christianity we will use the term "modernist." In a sense history is still taken very seriously by this kind of theologian. The
fundamentalist takes the actuality of all Biblical events seriously, and therefore attempts to elaborate a theology that asserts and conveys the religious meaning of the whole Bible.
The modernist can only treat with seriousness and reverence
those Biblical events the actuality of which he feels justified in
asserting as an honest historian, and it is the religious meaning
of these events which his theology asserts and conveys. Of
course the fundamentalist and the theologian differ enormously, but the modernist's attitude toward the few Biblical
episodes which he feels able to assert with integrity is remark-

ably like the fundamentalist's attitude toward all Biblical episodes.

The philosopher-theologian, however, may have a very different approach to the subject. The function of Biblical episodes,
whether actual or merely alleged, is, after all, to convey ideas.
Once the ideas have been conveyed it can make very little difference whether the episode that conveys them corresponded
to a past actuality or was no more than a somewhat shaky alle-
gation, for the really important question is not how we came
by our ideas but what is their value now we have them. Thus
to him, particularly if he is influenced by some kind of idealism,
or perhaps, in the twentieth century, by existentialist philosophy, the question of the actuality of Biblical events is of no
particular importance. This type of mind was perhaps best expressed in Lessing's famous dictum that it can never be permissible to base a universal religious truth on the occurrence of
a particular event. Such a philosopher-theologian as we are
considering at the moment seeks, after all, a Christianity of
pure, self-authenticating ideas rather than one implied by a
contingent course of past events, which, after all, can never be
too certain. In this book we shall term this approach to Christianity "liberal" and contrast it with modernism, although, as
we can clearly see, both belong to the same development of
thought and both are consequences of our two possible approaches to Christian theology, the philosophical or the historical, as they deal with a certain specific type of problem.

Thus the modernist produces what can only be called a drastically reduced type of Christianity, but at least he does cling
to the orthodox idea of the crucial character of historical actuality as the vehicle through which the divine revelation is
given. The liberal theologian is less at pains to reduce his Christianity. Indeed, as we can see in Loisy's famous L'évangile et
l'église, perhaps the ablest expression ever given to the liberal
spirit in theology, he need not be concerned to reduce it at all.
The significant element in his work is the tendency to remove
Christianity from its historical context. The result is that in

some ways Protestant modernism, even of an extreme variety, is closer to Catholic orthodoxy than the liberal Catholicism to be found in the Roman Church at the beginning of the century, and in Anglicanism particularly during the 1920's.

Historically speaking, it must be said that the two great classical Protestant Reformers were both of them profoundly orthodox. I use the word " orthodox " here in the strictest possible Christian sense. It refers to the results of the great classical, patristic discussions concerning the problems of Christology and the mystery of the Trinity. In this sense orthodoxy is to be found in the decisions of the great General Councils of the early church, and in the creeds that summarized their teaching. It is true that the appeal of the great Reformers was to Scripture, but in fact, of course, a pure appeal to Scripture is never possible. What the Biblical Christian appeals to is not mere or virgin Scripture, but Scripture interpreted in some particular way. The Protestant Reformers, like the Anglican reformers, believed — we might almost say took it for granted — that the true interpretation of Scripture is that which is to be found in the writings of the fathers of the early undivided church. In this sense of the word " orthodox," it must be said that classical Protestantism was permeated by a basic orthodoxy, and that to term the classical Protestants heretics was always to stretch the word beyond its proper meaning. Nevertheless, although the classical Protestants were not heretics, even from the Catholic point of view, it could be claimed that they deviated in significant ways from the authentic, central traditions of the church, and that in particular they departed from its modes of ministerial continuity, from its liturgical traditions and sacramental disciplines and beliefs. Whether they were right or wrong to do this is not for the moment in question here. It must, however, be admitted that they did do it, so that although in the strict sense of the word they cannot rightly be called heretics they must be pronounced deviants.

The two new Eucharistic theories, originating from within the Calvinist tradition but later gaining considerable hold upon

Lutherans, were virtualism and receptionism, and it is perhaps here that we find the germ of a certain indifference to the actuality of the event which the much later liberalism carries to its last logical consequence.

Undoubtedly both virtualism and receptionism were attempts to do justice to what would seem to be the profound religious values of the Catholic belief in the real presence of Christ in the Eucharist without postulating any actual Eucharistic event, such as was, for example, implied in the doctrine of transubstantiation. Of course, we must eat and drink bread and wine in the Eucharist in obedience to the Lord's command, and, of course, it is also true that at or in the context of the Eucharist the Lord really feeds the elect with his own redeeming vitality, but now this is no longer conceived of as occurring through the instrumentality of anything that actually happens to the bread and wine. In virtualism what we receive is not the body and blood of Christ but the virtue or redeeming value of the body and blood of Christ, and it is, after all, the virtue or value of the body and blood of Christ that really matters and avails. The bread is eaten and the wine is drunk as a mere act of obedience to the commandment of the Son of God. We cannot really say that the one necessitates the other, only that they have been joined together in external and arbitrary fashion because God so willed it. In all this, of course, the underlying philosophy is derived from the late medieval nominalism that gave the Reformers their intellectual training. Thus the value of the event is distinct and must be distinguished from the actuality of the event, and could conceivably be known and enjoyed apart from the event. Sooner or later somebody was bound to ask the question: " Why the event at all? Can we be right in supposing that God would clutter up this immense spiritual reality with a mere outward performance which in itself has no virtue whatever? "

Receptionism is closely related to virtualism. We would hazard the guess that all receptionists must also be virtualists, although it is not so clear that all virtualists must necessarily be receptionists. Nevertheless, given the virtualistic conception of the Eucharist, receptionism would seem to be a natural way of conceiving the manner in which the virtue of the body and blood of Christ is actually transmitted to the communicant. Receptionism is also a theory based upon late medieval nominalism, although at the same time it looks forward to the occasionalism of so many of the French Cartesians. Occasionalism is primarily a way of dealing with the mind-body problem. There is certainly an order of physical events that is closed and complete in itself; there is also an order of mental events that is also closed and complete in itself. From a Cartesian point of view, it would appear that these two orders are completely separate and can in no way interact. Yet it is certainly the case that there appears to be some kind of harmony or reciprocity between them. For example, when a physical event occurs like the collapse of the roof of a house a number of mental events also occur that enable men to cognize the collapse and take measures with regard to it. The physical event is not, however, the cause of the mental event, rather it is the occasion of the mental event, for God has so arranged our world and the minds within it that each physical event is duplicated by a related event in the mental sphere and vice versa. Thus we have two orders of events, each complete in itself and neither dependent upon the other, yet bound together in what Leibnitz was later on to term a pre-established harmony. The point is that whenever a physical event occurs the appropriate and reciprocal mental event occurs and vice versa.

In the case of the Eucharist the physical event is eating bread and drinking wine as the Lord has commanded. The reciprocal mental or spiritual event is the feeding of the elect with the virtue or value of the body wounded and the blood shed on Calvary for us men and for our salvation. Neither of these events is the cause of the other, but God has willed that they shall coincide in time, i.e., that the physical event shall be the occasion of the spiritual event. Again the connection between the two events is reduced to the mere arbitrary fact that God for his own inscrutable reasons has willed and commanded that the two should coincide. We look in vain for any reason that will explain why this must be so, but for this kind of theology God is always absolute will rather than absolute reason, so that there need be no necessary logical connection between events that invariably coincide according to the inscrutable dictates of God.

It is, of course, possible that Calvin was somewhat influenced in this matter by his doctrine of predestination, although it is difficult to demonstrate this influence conclusively from his writings. Clearly, however, from the Calvinistic point of view we have to take seriously the possibility that some of those who are not elected to eternal salvation may nevertheless eat the bread and drink the wine at the Eucharist. Receptionism is at least a theory that enables us to explain that when such people eat the bread and drink the wine at the Eucharist they are not to be thought of as therefore receiving the body and blood of Christ.

Thus in both these theories we see a disentangling of the spiritual realities, virtues, and values from the sheer actuality of the events. The values and virtues of the Eucharist come to us in close connection with the eating of bread and wine, but not through the bread which is eaten or the wine which is drunk, nor because or as the result of anything that God does to the bread and the wine. Such beliefs give rise to a type of mind that is prone to concentrate upon spiritual reality and to regard physical and historical actuality as having no essential part to play in the scheme of things. Rather, their strange connection with spiritual events in the Bible and the liturgy becomes an odd, inexplicable accident.

It was not difficult to move on at a later date to views according to which the spiritual virtues and values, the intellectual and existential power, of Christianity were similarly related to the events recorded in the Bible. In the life and spiritual experience of the church the great sacramental events play a part analogous to the role of the great historic events to which Scripture testifies. If it is possible to diminish the status of the event in the life of the church without in any way forfeiting the spiritual reality, it is perhaps possible to diminish the status of the event in the Bible itself without in any way forfeiting the spiritual values of divine revelation. If spirituality is related so externally to event in the Eucharist, might it not be equally external to the events even in the Bible itself?

We may add that the view of baptism developed by the sixteenth-century Anabaptists and the later Baptists must have had a similar effect. Baptism, according to this view, is the outward event that signalizes and declares inward conversion, but the inward conversion now precedes the outward event, which merely signalizes and declares it, and is of infinitely greater importance. Indeed there have been groups of Baptists who have gone so far as to declare that the actual physical event of baptism is not really essential at all. The Quakers and many later spiritual and intellectual Christian groups were to take the same view of all sacramental events.

We have thus briefly outlined what we take to be the roots of this particular type of treason within Christianity, which has been so characteristic of elite groups within Protestantism. Such sacramental doctrines as these embody a pattern of thought which, when transposed into the area of Biblical interpretation, renders men constantly on the watch for a purely spiritual meaning, robs them of any sense of the crucial character of the event, and certainly disposes them toward the view that spiritual meaning can always be disentangled from physical or historical events, and even that in this disentangled condition not only is nothing lost but something priceless is gained. The spiritual meaning manifests itself as pure, self-authenticating idea, so that now the historical criticism of the event no longer constitutes the slightest threat to it. Thus spiritual meaning establishes its final independence of events, so that a historical critique can no longer violate its validity. All this became clear especially in the nineteenth century and particularly in Germany, the country that above all others created and popularized the modern literary and historical criticism of the Scriptures. Certainly the literary and historical critique of the Scriptures is older than the rise of the Hegelian idealistic philosophy, but it was in alliance with Hegelian idealism that literary and historical criticism of the Bible gave birth to a new type of Protestant religiosity, which we have chosen to call modernistic whenever the inspiration is primarily historical and liberal whenever the inspiration is primarily philosophical. The modernist and liberal trend, however, are but twin aspects of a single mood and thought, and the two have a tendency to converge, so that the difference is not always so sharp and clear in general usage as our definitions would seem to imply.

The particular crisis for Protestantism brought about by the rise of the literary and historical criticism of Scripture has often, I think, been misunderstood. Clearly the nineteenth-century attitude toward Scripture points toward an entirely new kind of Protestantism. It has frequently and tritely been said that this is because Protestantism appeals to Scripture and must therefore be vitally influenced by any new way of understanding Scripture, whereas Catholicism, since its appeal is not to Scripture but to the teaching and traditions of the living church, is quite untouched by the so-called higher criticism, or at least not affected to anything like the same extent. I believe that this is a superficial judgment that is the cause of much misunderstanding. The appeal of Catholicism to Scripture is quite as basic and emphatic as the appeal of Protestantism to Scripture. Neither can contemplate this almost literal manhandling of divine Scripture unaffected and unmoved. In both Protestantism and Catholicism it is obvious that the living church has to teach and to appeal to Scripture in order to establish the validity of its teaching. Catholicism indeed must even appeal to Scripture in order to establish the truth that the living church is the proper and appropriate teacher of the faith.

Actually the problem does not arise in this area at all. Certainly the classical Protestantism appealed to Scripture, but, as we have already seen, it took it for granted that the true and appropriate interpretation of Scripture is to be found in the writings of the fathers of the early church. Here, of course, Catholicism agrees. Where they differ is around the question, What is that interpretation of Scripture which we find in the writings of the fathers? Here, of course, many differences arise, but at least both are agreed as to the ultimate court of appeal. Now if we substitute for the appeal to Scripture as interpreted in patristic exegesis, an appeal to Scripture as interpreted by the so-called higher critics of the last two centuries or so, one thing must become clear to us, and that is that we are making a quite different appeal. Scripture as interpreted by the fathers is one thing; Scripture as interpreted by modern criticism is quite another. Hence, the classical Protestantism that appeals to the former is an entirely different thing from the modern Protestantism that appeals to the latter, and it often becomes difficult even to pretend that the one is the lineal – it is certainly not the logical – successor of the other. The problem is every bit as acute for Catholicism as for Protestantism, and for both it is crucial. The Bible as now interpreted by the exclusively literary and historical method is not the same thing as the Bible as it was received by the previous ages of the church and as it is still received by the vast mass of Christian people.

Please note what I am not saying – I do not believe that the precritical ages were fundamentalist, nor do I believe that the vast mass of Christian people even now are fundamentalist. Fundamentalism as we know it today is neither the innocence of the criticism nor the absence of the criticism, rather, it is a subsequent reaction against the criticism, one that a sympathetic observer, however much he disagrees with it, can understand and even in a way approve. It is a way of reacting against a technique of receiving and expounding the word of God out of which no word of God ever seems to come, a reaction against a self-acclaimed, pure spirituality that does not in practice seem to produce any genuine spirituality at all.

We are using here a new distinction between the terms " the-

ological modernism " and " theological liberalism " which has
not, I think, been previously attached to them. Usually the
terms have been rather vaguely and imprecisely used, and often
more or less identified. As we would use the words now, modernism refers to the earlier consequences of this movement of
thought rather than to the later. Its tendency is to reduce the
amount of Scripture that can be seriously credited by the responsible historian, and then to declare that Christianity itself
must be reduced to the religious meaning and value of the few
episodes that have proved able to survive historical criticism.
The result in the nineteenth and early twentieth centuries was
a naturalistic, highly ethical and social interpretation of Christ
and the Christian gospel which had comparatively little genuine religious content and did little to commend itself to the
genuine faith and religious experience of the church as a whole.

We would attach the term " liberalism " to the later phases
of this movement of thought, which, as for example we see today in Bultmann and his followers, is highly critical of mere
modernism and endeavors to escape from the ineptitude and
spiritual vanity of a reductionist Christianity. I am aware that
this way of using the terms does not fit too well with established usage. For example, the movement surrounding Loisy
and Tyrrell in the Roman Catholic Church at the beginning of
the century has almost always been called modernist, whereas
I should call it liberal rather than modernist. My only excuse
for attempting this new distinction is that established usage is
so confused that it seems to call for some clarification and cor-
rection. Modernism, then, is theologically reductionist and historically positivist, whereas liberalism is theologically more
fully and profoundly Christian, at least in intent, and historically nonpositivist.

The liberal view tends to begin with a criticism of positivist
ideas about history. If the aim of history is merely to know precisely what happened as it happened, to echo a phrase of
Leopold von Ranke,[3] if it is the result of a purely disinterested,
unbiased inquiry without presuppositions of any kind, then

positive history is a quest for the impossible. We cannot hope for disinterested historical knowledge because the plain fact is that true knowledge is never altogether disinterested. The philosophical background of this criticism is frankly existentialist. According to this view, the search for a purely objective knowledge, in which man surveys the past and present of this world like a god, as though he himself were not in the world, is based upon a total misconception of man's intellectual relationship to his environment. Human knowledge is always and necessarily a knowledge from within, a knowledge that reflects the situation, passions, and limitations of the knower, and never merely a knowledge that reflects the objective outlines and contours of what is known. Kierkegaard applied this thesis to philosophy; there is a sense in which we can say that Einstein and his successors applied it to physics; now it only remains to apply it to history.

We may perhaps pause to question whether in fact this view is necessarily correct. From the point of view, at all events, of what we may call an Augustinian epistemology of science and history, what is attained as a result of the application of truly scientific and historical methods is in fact a kind of mystical participation in God's knowledge of the world. So that indeed objective knowledge has a certain Godlike quality, and man, through that specific kind of divine grace or illumination which aids him intellectually in precisely the same way as grace in the more ordinary sense of the word supplements and reinforces his will, really attains something like the kind of knowledge, disinterested and objective, with which God knows the world. For this kind of knowledge, as we cannot forbear to observe, has a moral and spiritual, as well as an intellectual, value. Thus the Christian philosopher, even at this point, may find himself highly critical of the existentialist attitude. Nevertheless it is the case that the liberal thinkers we are now considering did indeed arrive at the belief that a completely objective account of history, such as we find in both fundamentalist and positivist historical criticism, is neither possible nor even desirable, and thus the gap between objective history and man-made mythology is considerably narrowed. Thus a new point of view is established, a point of view according to which it makes very little difference whether some particular episode falls into the category of history or into the category of mythology. In either case the really important question is not so much whether or not it really happened as the question of its religious and existential meaning.

Contemporary liberalism thus puts a high value both on mythology and on existentialist philosophy. Its religious intentions are more profoundly Christian than those of the early modernists, but it still has the same tendency to fail to do justice to the Biblical reverence for the actuality of the historical fact. Both modernists and liberals are often men of great and deserved repute in the field of Biblical scholarship, and yet both seem rather distant from something that is basic to the whole Biblical point of view. In the Bible the actuality of the accomplished fact is reverenced, and the knowledge of it ardently desired, because the accomplished fact is something that God has done, and what we want to know is precisely what it is that God has done. The Biblical category is the category of divine action; whereas, of course, the normal historical category is the category of human action. There is a very big difference between the two, but at least both are agreed that the important thing for us is to obtain as precise and objective a knowledge as possible of what actually happened — the Biblical writers because they want to know God and the modern historians because they want to understand man. For the liberals, however, God can be quite as profoundly and appropriately symbolized by and revealed in a myth as in an actual event, so that the religious meaning and value of Biblical episodes become altogether independent of their actuality.

Of course, such writers do not mean by the word "myth" a mere untruth. On the contrary, myth is, above all, the characteristic way in which religious truth is communicated and conveyed. We may compare with this the category of fiction. In great fiction there is a genuine apprehension of life, a vision of what life is about, of the great overarching issues at stake in human existence which is contained and expressed in a narration of events which never actually took place, but which nevertheless communicate profound truth, often of a deeply religious character.

Good near-contemporary examples of the profoundly intellectual and religious quality of great fiction can be found in writers of genius like Dostoevsky and Kafka. Obviously their novels are filled with profound truth, yet, equally obviously, it is not historical truth. We may compare many examples of accurate historical research and narration, shall we say a learned thesis on the incidence of bubonic plague among teenagers in the cities of the Hanseatic League during the twelfth and thirteenth centuries, which, however painstaking, would probably communicate no profound existential or religious truth at all. It would not even attempt to, to do such a research justice. Thus there is a sense in which fiction may conceivably be truer than truth. All Christian thinkers, perhaps with the exception of very extreme fundamentalists, would agree that the Bible contains a great deal of mythological material, and we must, of course, add that in most of the pagan and pre-Christian religion that provided the religious context of the growth of Biblical faith the category of myth reigns alone as almost the sole religious category. Thus we arrive at the view that religion is inherently mythological, or, to put it another way, that the characteristic form of religious speech and communication is mythic.

In this chapter our concern is to show how these developments came about rather than to criticize them. Criticism will come later, but we must note even here that this notion raises for us one acutely difficult question. Granted that there is such a thing as religious speech, and even granted that religious speech is characteristically mythic, we have still to ask ourselves the question whether Christianity is in fact a religion, and whether in consequence, the characteristically religious forms of speech will suffice for the communication of Christianity. Briefly to anticipate what must be said in more detail at a later stage, I would hold (1) that Christianity is not a religion in the ordinary sense of the word and (2) that in consequence the ordinary and accepted forms of religious speech, though no doubt they may be appropriately used by Christianity at different times, cannot suffice for the communication of Christianity itself.

Certainly the early Christians did not believe that the speech in terms of which they communicated the gospel was mythic. In the Gentile world they were face to face with forms of religious proclamation which were quite frankly mythic, and they laid their stress precisely upon the great distinguishing characteristic of Christianity, i.e., that whereas other forms of religion used mythic speech, they, in proclaiming the gospel, were using historic speech. Here of course they displayed how profoundly Biblical and Hebraic was their entire point of view. The Christian masses are now indoctrinated with this point of view, precisely because it was for so many centuries the point of view of the Christian elites. Certainly one consequence of the contemporary abandonment of this point of view by so many of the Christian elites is to undermine the vast historic and historically effective distinction between the Christian gospel, on the one hand, and pagan mythology in general and the Greek mystery religions in particular, on the other hand. Thus the treason of the contemporary Christian elites is this fateful abandonment of what was, from the very beginnings of Christian proclamation, the great differentia of Christianity from all forms of what I would call mere religion.

The second great difficulty about these contemporary liberal theological movements is a revival, in a new form, of course, of the double truth theory that had so much influence during the high Middle Ages. Once more we are told, in many different ways, that something can be true in the order of religious thought, and valid and relevant in the process of religious communication, which from some other and much more ordinary and widespread point of view is not true at all. The result is the prevalence of a kind of theological gobbledygook or double talk which resembles nothing so much as the famous "double think" of George Orwell's *1984*. Here are a few examples of actual remarks uttered in my presence during theological conversation with highly intelligent colleagues: "John wrote the Fourth Gospel theologically, but not as a matter of historical fact." "Mary was not a physical virgin; she was a spiritual virgin." "Christ did not actually rise from the dead; the belief that he did is a measure of the tremendous impression that he made on the minds of the disciples, so that we can affirm the resurrection theologically but not historically." "The resurrection means that new life is an existential possibility for every one of us now." "We must live as *if* we believed Christ rose from the dead, because this is the best way of passing from inauthentic to authentic personal existence." Now I believe that statements of this kind can never be taken seriously by mass thought and that the contemptuous way in which the Christian, and indeed non-Christian, masses sweep aside such utterances of the Christian elites as these is amply justified. This may or may not be a good way of communicating religion, but it is a very bad way indeed of communicating Christianity. The Christian claim has been so different from the religious claim, and for so long, that if this kind of thing is indeed genuinely religious language it is certainly not now any kind of Christian language at all. Indeed, as I have said already, it never has been from the very beginning.

Mass Christianity and, until very recently, elite Christianity, is at least Biblical enough to reverence and treat with the utmost seriousness the actuality of the event. It is a strange paradox that, out of a great and commendable preoccupation with the Bible and with the interpretation of Scripture, so many of the Christian elites have achieved a point of view that estranges them from the Biblical point of view almost entirely. All this is, as I have said, a mere anticipation of the critique of this point of view which will be attempted later in this book.

For the moment we must note that the liberal Christian elites have now placed themselves in a situation in which it is almost impossible for them to say anything intelligible to, or anything that will be taken seriously by, the Christian masses at all, to say nothing of the non-Christian masses who are most unlikely to be evangelized by such a faltering witness as this.

It is perhaps well that by no means all the Christian elites are of this liberal persuasion, so that the authentic Christianity still finds elite expression from intellectuals and scholars who have not broken in the same way with the essential Christian tradition, who still conduct an apologetic ministry on behalf of the authentic Christian tradition which is in harmony with the evangelistic witness to that tradition and in close and sympathetic touch with the wisdom and validity of mass thought. Elites of this kind are to be found today in the revived, often scholarly and intellectual, fundamentalism on the one hand, and in Catholicism upon the other. It is interesting to notice how very closely these two converge together. But more significant is the fact that both converge so closely with the wisdom and validity of mass thought that they are capable of both apologetic and evangelistic effectiveness at the same time and with complete intellectual integrity.

Another area of weakness in the elite outlook, which we have been chronicling here rather than criticizing, is the strange and paradoxical vogue in this style of thought of both philosophical naturalism and philosophical existentialism at the same time. But the criticism of these two forms of philosophy, and of their influence upon contemporary Christian elites, must await a later chapter. For the moment the time has now come for a careful analysis of the wisdom and validities of mass thought, to which we must immediately turn.

Chapter III

The Sanity of the Masses

Like folk art and folklore, mass thought is essentially anonymous. Indeed there is a sense in which the very term " mass thought " is a misnomer, for nobody really thinks mass thought. The attempt to exhibit the genius of mass thought in some kind of considered philosophical system is an activity not of the masses but of a sympathetic and discerning elite philosophy. Since mass thought cannot think itself, it is incapable also of defining and defending itself; so that the masses desperately need the services of the elite philosophers who are the proper defenders of their sanity. Mass thought just is wherever the masses are, informing their action and shaping and dictating their instinctive judgments.

One reason why so many elite philosophers sweep aside mass thought with contempt is that so many of the particular mass judgments which emerge out of mass thought are so obviously wrong. The masses are credulous and superstitious, prone to the repetition of baseless traditional shibboleths. Criticism is not their strong suit, so that the sense of intellectual superiority which rises so easily in the minds of elite thinkers is not altogether surprising and sometimes even forgivable. If the only possible virtue of a system of thought is that it should produce a maximum number of accurate particular judgments and a minimum of particular errors, then certainly we cannot rate mass thought very highly. If we would understand and sympathize with its virtues, we must seek them elsewhere.

What mass thought does succeed in grasping and conveying so well is a sense of the breadth and variety of experience, a broad command of its great and valid forms. No doubt in every valid area or form of experience gross mistakes will occur, but the mistakes do not void the form of its validity. Elite thought has been too concerned with the necessity of avoiding error, so that it is apt to dismiss forms of experience in terms of which a high proportion of error occurs as totally invalid, but this is not necessarily so. Despite hallucination and physical illusion, perception is still regarded by most of us in theory and by all of us in practice as a valid form of experience, conveying to us a genuine relationship to a world external to ourselves. Of course a certain proportion of what passes for perception consists of illusion and error, but this does not affect the validity of perception itself. Illusion can only occur as a misperception of a real world. Man may misperceive or misconceive the real, but he never succeeds in either perceiving or conceiving the totally unreal. (He can, of course, conceive *that* the totally unreal might appear but not *what* it could be like.)

Thus it is foolish to argue, as some philosophers have done in the past, that because of the occurrence of hallucination and illusion, perception itself is untrustworthy. Even if illusion and hallucination occurred much more frequently than in fact they do, it would still be true that perception itself remains a valid form of experience. The same thing is true of other areas of experience, for example, the existential experience of the dynamic self, religious experience, imaginative experience, and so on. Doubtless in these areas illusion is even more common, but the form of the experience remains valid despite the high incidence of error. Indeed we may even be grateful for the credulity of the masses, for at least this tends to preserve the form of the experience itself.

Modern elite thought has tended to substitute for a careful and discriminating critique of the actual judgments and affirmations that occur within a form of experience a critique, not of the alleged experiences, but of the form of the experience itself, with the object of establishing its total or blanket nonvalidity. In so doing, it tends to impoverish life and to destroy its rich and stimulating variety. For example, there can be no doubt that an enormous number of alleged experiences of the miraculous and supernatural are erroneous and due to the uncritical credulity with which the mass of mankind throw themselves into such forms of experience, but this is no reason for declaring that the form of the experience as such is invalid; from which it would follow that not a great many but all reports of experience of this form are necessarily erroneous. What we want is a criticism of the details rather than a critique of the generalities. There is no area of experience which is exempt from error. Errors occur in science, in historical research, and everywhere else. Indeed it is no doubt true that in their earlier and cruder phases science and historical research produced many more erroneous than valid judgments. It is fortunate that nobody supposed at that time that this demonstrated the nonvalidity of these forms of experience and inquiry. Even the erroneous judgments help to keep alive and preserve the immense potentialities of the empirical form and thus to keep our minds constantly open to the many-sidedness of reality.

Thus the first great virtue of mass thought, demanding our profound appreciation, is this openness of the mind to reality, this almost naïve responsiveness to the richness and variety of the forms of experience, this comparative absence of skepticism. We may describe this as the realism of mass thought. In elite philosophy the term " realism " has changed its meaning. In the Platonic tradition, for example, realism connoted a certain transcendental actuality of the universal: in nominalism and later eighteenth-century empiricism it referred, above all, to the immediate actuality of the sensed particular; or, to put it another way, Platonic realism stressed the validity of conception whereas modern empirical realism has laid its emphasis on the validity of perception. The general tendency of the history of elite thought has been to play off these two forms of realism against each other: the Platonists distrusting sense experience, the empiricists distrusting what they regard as abstract and speculative ideas. One of the great virtues of mass thought is its tendency to embrace both forms of realism at the same time, to acknowledge in Platonic fashion the realities that cannot be sensed and in empirical fashion the reality of what can be sensed. As a result it approximates toward what might be called a total realism, which agrees with the affirmations of both Platonic and empirical realism at the same time, remaining skeptical of their denials.

This leads us to the second great virtue of mass thought: its distrust of antitheses and dilemmas. Self-consciously logical, elite thought is particularly fond of the method of tracing antitheses between concepts, so that it can argue again and again that because one thing is true some other thing must be false, above all, that because one form of experience is valid some additional or alternative form of experience must be invalid. Modern philosophy, whether pure or applied, has abounded in controversies in which reasoning of this kind has been resorted to; for example: the reason or revelation dilemma, the science or religion controversy, the endless logical arguments about external and internal relations, and so on. A man once asked me, "Which is the more important, eating or drinking?" I could reply only that we should certainly die if we totally neglected either. I merely narrate the episode as an amusing example of the obvious fallacy of the either-or method in philosophy. We can see clearly enough that its great danger is the impoverishment of thought, the truncation of experience, the narrowing of our capacity for recognition and response. In this sense mass credulity is intellectually superior to rational skepticism because it at least preserves the great potentialities of the manifold forms of experience.

We transfer the principle of noncontradiction too easily from the areas of experience to which it belongs to other areas in which it is less obviously at home. For example, if I spent last night at the opera it is clear that I did not spend it in the home of my friend Mr. Smith. It is obvious that this must indeed be the case. We cannot say, on the other hand, that a similar relationship holds good as between distinctive forms of experience: for example, that if I am capable of scientific thought and research, I must therefore be incapable of saying my prayers; that, in other words, if I am a scientist, I cannot be a religious man; and, conversely, if I am a religious man, I cannot really be a scientist. Of course a position like this can be argued, or even taken for granted, but it has neither the immediacy nor the cogency of my earlier example and the logical value of the one example should not be attributed to the other.

Note that in all this I am not contending for any kind of irrationalism. I am not arguing that elite thought is too rationalistic whereas mass thought relies upon profounder intuitions. The only kind of rationalism against which I should protest is a narrowing, insensitive rationalism that is not rational enough. I would not even agree to the implied antithesis between reason and intuition, for what, after all, is a process of reasoning but a chain of intuitions? And what, after all, is an intuition but a single moment in a process of rational thought; or in what is at least capable of being laid bare as a process of rational thought? Otherwise the intuition is a mere vague and baseless impression or hunch.

On the other hand, there is this also to be said: men were rational long before they were conscious of rationalism, just as they ate and drank, breathed, walked and ran, reproduced their kind, matured, aged, and died long before they had any conscious physiological theory. Rationalism is rather like the man who was surprised to learn that he had been talking prose all his life. Rationalistic man consciously studies a kind of cerebration which has been characteristic of man ever since he has been man. Reason is first of all in the event and only subsequently identified and defined as such in the mind. This means that reason informs mass thought, is pregnant and potential in human society, history, and culture long before its presence is detected, analyzed, and celebrated by the elite thinker. Unless mass thought possessed this informing rationality, no elite thought could ever emerge out of human history to inform us about it. Thus elite thought is historically continuous with mass thought. Its rationalism is the refinement of a datum, not the invention of some new elite expedient. For elite thought to content itself with merely destructive critiques of the forms of mass thought is to cut itself off from its roots, industriously to sever the branch upon which it is still precariously perched.

Some recognition of this is to be found in the writings of the linguistic analysts, who have taken the place on the contemporary philosophical scene once filled by the logical positivists. Their method is to select some ordinary remark or trite cliché frequently heard in mass conversation and subject it to a careful analysis that indicates that it presupposes, betrays, or implies their own general point of view, with the object of showing that their philosophy is simply the articulation of the more confused intuitions of mass thought. One of the best and most persuasive examples of this method is Gilbert Ryle's *The Concept of Mind*. This book is weak on history but plausible and even good in many other ways, and far more consonant with Biblical and Christian thought than Ryle imagines. He seems to think that all men and all philosophers were Cartesians long before Descartes, which is a gross error of historical perspective, but once we have allowed that historical perspective is not Ryle's strong point there is much in his exposition that is both profitable and enjoyable. The weakness of the method, however, is that it assumes that mass thought is much more articulate than in fact it is, and that common speech chronicles its intuitions far more accurately and definitively than is in fact the case.

Mass thought is better comprehended sociologically through an examination of the many-sided cultures and the variety of institutions characteristic of man's history than through this painstaking analysis of the clichés of common speech. The mass man uses his words loosely and ambiguously. The characteristic of mass thought is not so much that it says this or that in particular as that it entertains so many forms of experience at the same time, within the same culture, within the same life-time, within the orbit of a single perceptive mind. Thus the anthropologist studying a single, simple society, narrow in its range of experience, minute in scale, inevitably restricted in its outlook, can trace within that complex the immense potentialities of religion and science, of economics and the arts, of morality and romance, of the life of the imagination and the life of reason. The scale is minute but the human complexity is nevertheless almost infinite, and this complexity of experience is one of the essential characteristics of men. Perhaps indeed, in the last analysis, that which differentiates the human from everything else that we find in the creation is this rich complexity which mass thought so faithfully and excitingly represents. Elite rationalistic movements, on the other hand, often endeavor to restore a lost simplicity which, in fact, was never really lost, because it was never really there to lose in the first place.

Since the important work of the great philologists of the late nineteenth century, especially, of course, Max Müller, there has been a particular interest in the effect of various groups or systems of language upon the thought of those who use them. Certainly language does exercise a very important influence upon forms of thought. Language is not merely the means through which we communicate our thoughts, it is also the medium in which we think them, even those which we do not subsequently communicate. Language is certainly much more than a mere means of communication. It is also true, however, that thought exerts a reciprocal influence upon language. Language is never a merely fixed system but always a growing and developing one, so that while language is influencing thought, thought is also influencing language. It would certainly be a mistake to exhibit thought as a mere puppet of language. Of course, some forms of language may frustrate and inhibit some forms of thought, so that we can never say that the thought of a people is entirely laid bare in the forms of its language, and thinking is always more than the mere analysis and exploitation of the potentialities of a language, which is perhaps what some of our so-called "ordinary language boys" working in present-day philosophy would make it. For the purposes of thought indeed all existing languages are taken to be more or less inadequate, and in the past, philosophy has been a kind of sustained protest and rebellion against the limitations of its linguistic instrument. It is thanks at least in part to generations of dead philosophers that we have now learned to use our language to think and to communicate many thoughts which would at one time have been incommunicable and indefinable. Philosophy is always in part a raid upon the inarticulate, an adventure beyond the limitations of speech, which makes speech sovereign over new and hitherto unknown territories.

One example of this alleged influence of speech upon thought is the distinction between languages that are rich in nouns and adjectives and therefore supposed to conduce to a type of thought that lays its stress upon substance and the continued being of more or less permanent entities, and another kind of language that is particularly rich in verbs and therefore lays its stress upon continuing processes and patterns of development and change. No doubt the distinction has something in it, but we must beware of pushing it too far. There is no language that is entirely lacking in verbs, on the one hand, or in nouns and adjectives on the other. All peoples, in fact, recognize both the being of entities and the actuality of processes. We can trace here different degrees of emphasis but not an antithesis.

Various brands of twentieth-century process philosophy have laid particular stress on evolving systems, but the kind of philosophy that would deny the being of entities and embrace only developmental processes and patterns of change is an elite sophistication, and certainly not the characteristic hallucination of any form of mass thought whatsoever. For a process philosopher, for example, the being of a stone would become the process of being a stone and by analogy the being of men becomes the process of being a human. For mass thought, how-

ever, these two categories are far from being antithetical. The
entity is always the natural subject of the activity; the activity
is either performed by or occurs to or within the entity. Mass
thought, to employ the theme of one of A. N. Whitehead's most
famous works, acknowledges both process and reality, and
traces no antithesis between the two.

No doubt the general tendency of the process philosophers
was to prefer the biological to the physical sciences. They tried
to escape from mere mechanism by interpreting physics in
terms of biology rather than the other way round. Religious
thinkers jumped rather naively to the conclusion that vitality
is closer to spirituality than mechanism, and often tended to
welcome the change. Vitality, they supposed, was dynamic,
whereas the alternative to the process philosophy was felt to
be a static universe and a static god. This certainly provided
modern religious philosophers with a philosophical ground for
tinkering with accepted forms of religious thought, which acknowledge, as indeed does mass thought, both entity and process, both static and dynamic concepts, and see in God the ultimate fusion of the two, complete and eternal in his perfection,
ever active in his love, in creation, redemption, and sanctification. In authentic Christian orthodoxy God is no more merely
static than merely dynamic but a rich synthesis of the two.
There is both an entity of the Godhead and the process of the
creative, redemptive divine action. The entity is no mere hy-
postatization of the process, nor is the process the total manifestation of the entity. The God made manifest in the divine
action remains in the profoundest sense the unknown God, a
well of being both hidden and revealed in his activity.

A good contemporary example of a form of language not indeed rich in anything, but, at all events, much more adequately
supplied with nouns and adjectives than with verbs, is the so-
called "Basic English," which improvises its verbs by com-
pounding nouns and adjectives with the verbs "to have" and
"to be." Certainly anyone who has tried to use the clumsy
translation of the New Testament into Basic English published

some years ago will have felt that this is a most frustrating experience, even for a thinker who is credited with trying to do
his thinking in the supposedly static forms of Greek and classical European philosophical thought. Basic English, of course,
is an artificial and improvised instrument of communication,
not really language at all. Certainly no real language is so poor
in verbs as Basic English. All real languages attempt in some
way or other to do justice to both process and reality. If we try
to imagine some artificial language at the opposite extreme to
Basic English in which we have a profusion of verbs and prac-
tically no nouns or adjectives at all, apart from present par-
ticiples, verbal nouns, or the names of processes, we can see at
once that we should experience a similar frustration. We should
certainly have a vivid experience of the way in which the intuitions of mass thought rebel against the threadbare antitheses of the elites, who so superfluously play off one category
against another and are so chronically prone to perceive con-
tradictions where there are none.

This linguistic phase of the question is of peculiar importance for contemporary theological discussion because of the
stress that is nowadays laid by so many thinkers on the difference between Greek language and Hebrew language, and consequently between Greek thought and Hebrew thought.[4] Of
course, the idea in itself is by no means new. Harnack, in his
famous *History of Dogma*, attempted to describe the development of early Christian thought on the assumption that it was
the story of a progressive deterioration of the original gospel of
Jesus as a result of the necessity of rethinking it in alien Hellenistic terms. Catholic Christianity, according to Harnack, was
the triumph of the Greek over the Hebrew mind, and Greek
thought, so extravagantly praised at the time of the Renaissance, and since then of course up to our own day, was suddenly revealed as the villain of the piece. Now, of course, the
theory has been well articulated as the result of many later contributions. Greek thought, we are told, is more impressed by

the reality of space, Hebrew thought by the reality of time; Greek thought is dominated by a dualistic distinction between mind and body, whereas Hebrew thought insists on the absolute unity of the two; Greek thought is static, whereas Hebrew thought is dynamic; and so on. Where the antithesis is developed to an extreme, Greek thought is exhibited as rationalistic; Hebrew thought, as revelational and intuitive.

There can be no doubt, of course, that there is a real and significant distinction between the two, but again we must protest against the erection of any sharp antithesis. Obviously we have here an instance of the occurrence within the specialized realm of Christian theology of the distinction we have already made between mass thought and elite thought. Hebrew thought represents mass thought, whereas Greek thought represents elite thought. Thus Hebrew thought is not something that any Hebrew ever thought. Hebrew thought as expounded in some coherent system is the work of the modern student and interpreter of Hebrew literature. Our knowledge of Greek thought, however, is the result of a careful study of the writings of Greek philosophers. We are comparing not silent Hebrews with articulate Greeks, but articulate Greeks with equally articulate modern interpreters of Hebrew. Thus the two are not altogether comparable, nor can they too lightly be played off against each other. Of one thing we can be sure: even if it is true that Greek thinkers preferred spatial to temporal categories, they were certainly nevertheless vividly aware that there is such a thing as time; conversely, even though it may be true that the Hebrews were more impressed by time than by space, this certainly does not mean that they were unimpressed by the reality of space, and similarly all along the line of demarcation which is supposed to mark out this fateful antithesis. Recent books on this subject, particularly those by Thorleif Boman [5] and Claude Tresmontant,[6] both modify the antithesis in significant ways. The truth would appear to be that Hebrew thought was strong where Greek thought was weak, and conversely. It is this which made possible the unique achievement of patristic Christian thought in hammering out a genuine and creative synthesis of the two.

In the Christian church, beginning with Paul, we see a persistent disinclination to take sides in any kind of struggle between Hebrew thought and Greek thought or to play one off against the other. For Paul, whose intellectual training and habits of thought would certainly place him on the Hebrew rather than on the Greek side of this great divide, both Greek and Hebrew thought, considered as closed systems deriving their inspiration solely from their own potentialities, must be pronounced inadequate from the Christian point of view, and both are incapable of grasping the essence of Christianity. The Christ is "unto the Jews a stumblingblock, and unto the Greeks foolishness" (I Cor. 1:23, KJV). Christianity is neither merely Greek nor merely Hebrew but beyond both, and therefore an intellectual milieu in which each can be enriched with the treasures of the other. We may say that the whole development of Christian thought and theology through the patristic period is a vindication of Paul's judgment. In this age of the creeds and the councils Christianity becomes Greek in its modes of expression and forms of systematization while remaining unchangeably Hebrew in its substance. In the words of Charles Williams, "The gospel became a creed without ceasing to be a gospel."

What we sometimes forget is the extent to which the golden age of Greek thought had become a matter of past history by the time that Christianity launched its evangelical attack on classical civilization. The great age of Socrates and Plato and Aristotle was three or more centuries away, and the Greek rationalism of the Christian Era no longer had the inspiration of a subject matter and theme worthy of its analytic and expressive power. Christianity provided Greek thought with a totally new and inspiring theme, so that we may think of the patristic age as a kind of classical Indian summer, the last phase of the glory leading up to moments, for example, in

Augustine, which recall and rival the power and penetration of Plato and Aristotle themselves. The result of this development was a Christian intellectualism that was neither altogether Greek nor altogether Hebrew, but in a sense greater and more creative than either because it contained the riches of both. It would certainly appear that the attempt of many modern theologians since Harnack to do what the primitive and patristic church carefully refrained from doing, that is, play off Greek thought against Hebrew thought, is a most untimely development. If it were to be done at all, it should have been done early; certainly it is now much too late.

If for the moment we conceive Hebrew thought as mass thought and Greek thought as elite thought, the great achievements of the patristic age clearly reinforce the general thesis that informs this book. The proper relationship between elite thought and mass thought is one of synthesis rather than antithesis, and this synthesis is the characteristic mark of the highest achievement of elite thought. Elite thought, as we see it in the very greatest of the early Christian fathers, is not a smug and self-conscious intellectual superiority that demonstrates its excellence in a clever mockery of mass thought. Rather, it is an articulation of mass thought providing it with definitive modes of expression which make possible an elucidating of its presuppositions and an ascertaining of its implications.

The achievement of Christian elite thought in the patristic age may be described as the hammering out of an orthodoxy that is an elite articulation of the Christianity of those masses of Christian people who must at all times constitute the great majority both in church and civilization. We are confronted with a rational exposition and interpretation and intellectual apologetic which is at all times in harmony with the evangelical proclamation that prompts and stimulates the response of faith and with the life of faith which is so evangelically aroused. Thus any kind of schism between a "high-brow" apologetic, elite Christianity and a "low-brow" mass Christianity is avoided, and the intellectual integrity of the church jealously preserved. It is perhaps no exaggeration to say that this kind of basic intellectual unity within Christendom was not to be threatened again until after the rise of nominalism, though we can perhaps trace something of the kind in the early medieval prejudice of the so-called antidialectics against the work of the great philosopher-theologians of the Scholastic period.

It is still true, however, that Christian orthodoxy is at the same time both a mass movement and an elite refinement, and in this sense we may claim with G. K. Chesterton that Christian orthodoxy is a profoundly democratic thing in the best sense of the word. The trouble is, of course, that the word "democratic" is nowadays put to so many corrupt uses that it has become almost meaningless. To the modern ear it is now little more than a vague synonym for a great good that does little to specify any particular form or mode of goodness. If, however, we mean by cultural democracy some high degree of convergence and solidarity between elites and masses, then we may surely claim that Christian orthodoxy was and is one of the greatest democratic achievements that the world has ever seen.

Part of our trouble is that, as a result of so many of the corruptions and backslidings of history, what we now think of as democracy and the liberal way of life have been established in so many countries as the result of modern revolutions, so that people have come to regard them as characteristically modern ideas and achievements rather than as a late flowering of ancient seeds. It is perhaps at this point that the English experience (and the English mind which it has fostered) is able to make its greatest contribution to the modern world's understanding of itself. It has been the great and, it must be admitted, totally undeserved good fortune of the English people to move slowly into their constitutional democracy and liberal way of life without the aid of the violent and narrowly rationalistic revolutions of the eighteenth, nineteenth, and twentieth centuries which have occurred in so many other parts of the world. In the English experience liberalism and democracy are ancient and medieval rather than modern institutions. From this point of view personal freedom to think, speak, and act are aristocratic virtues, at long last made available to the many other social groups. Democracy, government by discussion rather than violence, in which the free man respects the free man because only so can he hope that his own freedom will be respected, is again a state of common well-being which can be discerned in the mutual respect with which members of aristocratic groups approach one another. We hear so much about baronial and feudal wars in the Middle Ages that we often forget the more normal period of nonwar which even those stormy periods in human history regarded as more characteristic of themselves at their best.

Similarly the liberal way of life is that which for the ancient world characterized the mutual intercourse of free men in a world in which most men were slaves. Modern democracy means that now we are all regarded as free men, so that we can all enter into the fullness of the ancient aristocratic inheritance. We have achieved that state of affairs, which was such a nightmare to the Duke of Plaza-Toro, in which everybody is somebody, and we have particularly to beware of transforming it into a period in which nobody is anybody. We are most likely to avoid this tragic reduction of the promise of democracy to a new kind of social totalitarianism if we remain aware of the great debt of modern democracy to classical thought and the aristocratic Middle Ages.

Democracy, in other words, is the masses' entering into the heritage of the elite. We have to beware of inverting this historical relationship and producing a parodied, illiberal democracy in which the elites are reduced at last to the servile status of the ancient masses. Certainly from this point of view we can appreciate the emergence of Christian orthodoxy during the patristic period as perhaps the first truly great and truly democratic achievement that characterizes our cultural history. Certainly the danger of a democracy that emerges merely out of revolution is that it may become a rootless thing, so irrelevant to the human past that it may have all too little to say to the human future. If democracy and the liberal way of life are indeed by revolution, then, it must be added, in the language of the racing stud, " that they are by revolution out of tradition," so that both the conservative and the radical mind may feel a sense of paternal pride as they look at what has emerged out of their mutual efforts.

Nevertheless, mass thought and its proper and indeed indispensable contribution to cultural democracy are in constant danger, perhaps especially in our contemporary world. As we have already seen, just as elite thought is corrupted by sophistication, so mass thought is overthrown by brutalization. The brutalization of mass thought is not due to speculative materialism but rather to a certain kind of instinctive, unthought sensationalism and earthiness. Of course, all mass thought takes sense data and the characteristic earthiness of the human creature with extraordinary seriousness. At its best, however, mass thought takes other things with equal seriousness, so that for mass thought to concentrate on sense data and the earthiness of man to the exclusion of other things which it formerly stressed is to reduce that characteristic breadth of content, that wide openness to experience, which has historically been its finest characteristic.

The brutalization of mass thought is, from one point of view, a reaction against sophisticated elite thought. Sophisticated elite thought has failed to grasp the richness and potentialities of mass thought. Mass thought, no doubt assisted to a considerable extent by popular education, which refines the masses by communicating to them a small assortment of elite methods and concepts, without of course transforming the masses into elites, responds by artificially simplifying them in the hope that new types of elite sophistication will achieve a new relationship with the masses in this brutalized condition. To some extent signs are not lacking that this stratagem is enjoying considerable success. Thus elite thought in the nineteenth century most prevalently took the form of sophisticated idealism which either criticized or ignored the sensationalistic and earthy elements in mass thought. Now, however, although there is still very little elite materialism, we are confronted with that peculiar kind of materialism characteristic of the Marxists and called dialectical; and from the same quarter, with merely economic interpretations of history, with various brands of philosophical and linguistic positivism, with varieties of pragmatism or instrumentalism, and with the so-called process philosopher who knows nothing characterized by the dignity of being.

It is obvious that all these are highly sophisticated types of elite thought, yet at the same time it can also be said that they converge upon a new relationship to mass thought in its brutalized condition; for in this brutalized form, mass thought is at least sufficiently simple and shallow for the elite thinker to be able to express it in his favorite manner as a series of antitheses and dilemmas enabling him to assert something or other at the cost of the denial of something else. In other words, in its brutalized form, mass thought has lost its great intellectual comprehensiveness, its capacity for broad and varied affirmation, its responsiveness to life and experience in its extraordinary richness and variety, so that in this brutalized form the sophisticated elites can find themselves at home with it once more.

How far is this prevalent brutalization of mass thought due to the extraordinary vogue of the natural sciences in contemporary culture? Many of our elites, who are particularly drawn to the study of the humanities, are apt to draw a picture of the contemporary cultural civilization in which the sciences appear as the villains of the piece. It seems to me that such an interpretation requires drastic qualification. We have to remember that for the most part our modern masses are as little acquainted with the sciences as with the humanities. It is certainly true that our mass media of modern education do a poor job so far as the humanities are concerned; it is even more notorious that their failure with regard to the sciences is, if anything, even greater. We are apt to call this a scientific age, but that certainly does not mean that ours is a time in which the majority of people have any understanding of the achievements and the values of the scientist. On the contrary, there is remarkably little understanding of the sciences. It is a commonplace among educationalists that few subjects are so badly taught in our schools as mathematics, that essential handmaid of science. Galileo tells us in a famous phrase that "mathematics is the language in which the book of nature is written." We can only comment that, if this is so, remarkably few of us seem likely ever to read it.

It is indeed because of the extraordinary importance of mathematics in the sciences in general and in the physical sciences in particular that it can truly be said that the general tendency of modern science and philosophy is to lead us back to something very like the conceptual realism of Plato. For the man whose philosophical outlook is particularly inspired and guided by the condition and tendency of twentieth-century physics, something very like the Platonic outlook seems to be very close to the truth. There is a perceptual world we live and experiment in and a conceptual, primarily mathematical, world we think in; and the still rather obscure relationship between these two worlds is such that the more profoundly we enter into the depths of the mathematical world we think in, the more creatively we are enabled to interpret and understand and manipulate the sensed objects — sensed either by us or by our more sensitive and perceptive instruments — which confront us in the world in which we live. The resulting philosophical account of the two worlds need not, of course, be dualistic. It is doubtful if it was really dualistic even in Plato himself. It can still be argued that in an even deeper sense these two distinguishable but not truly distinct worlds nevertheless constitute one world. This is obviously the point of view of the Nicene Creed; at least possibly the point of view of Plato; there is certainly no reason why it should not be the point of view also of the modern philosopher of science.

If we are in any way to blame science for the brutalization

of contemporary mass thought, it is the prevalent misunderstanding rather than understanding of science which must bear the brunt of the criticism. The real source of the trouble is the enormous vogue of the sciences in an intellectual and cultural milieu which is quite incapable of understanding them. To the great mass of our contemporaries science is simply the extraordinary technical achievements and powers to which we have become accustomed in the contemporary world. The scientist has become today a kind of wonder-worker or medicine man, the steward of those processes which men cannot understand but upon which they feel their welfare to depend. For the modern mass man science simply is what it manifestly does. Now it would be much nearer the truth to say that science is what it thinks and understands rather than to say that it is what it does. The technological deeds of science are no more than a kind of froth surrounding its intrinsic excellence. Of course we may take the deeds of science as sacramental symbols of its real intellectual achievement, but to take them as the substance of science itself is utterly unfair to both science and the scientists. Thus, in so far as science enters at all into our account of the prevalent brutalization of mass thought, it is the popular misunderstanding rather than the popular understanding of science which is the true cause of our trouble.

Actually the brutalization of mass thought, the obsession with process and function, so that everything is in the world to be used and nothing is there to be honored and adored, the preoccupation with the vivid sense datum, so that reality becomes something that requires to be sensed rather than comprehended, was possible and often actual long before the days of modern science. After all, the brutalization of mass thought resembles the sophistication of elite thought in at least one significant way. Both are attempts to evade the extraordinary complexity and embarrassing richness of life and reality. Both are attempts to foist upon the creation an artificial simplicity that, when openly experienced at first hand, it does not possess. If only we can succeed in explaining away vast elements of our experience, the residue can be composed into a simpler pattern of reality, less challenging intellectually and less of a burden existentially. Thus, from this point of view, all that is required to adjust the sophistication to the brutalization is for the sophisticated form of thought to move away from idealism, which achieves its artificial simplicity by denying or explaining away the physical and naturalistic elements of experience, to a sensationalistic and quasi-materialistic form of thought which achieves a similar simplification by denying or explaining away the mental and spiritual elements of experience. The latter expedient possesses the great advantage of making possible a new harmony between elite and mass thought. It is obvious that mass thought will never go in the idealistic direction, but elite thought can perhaps be persuaded to embrace a physicalist and sensationalist outlook on life. If the elites will not or cannot lead, let them at least follow. In the words of the popular cliché, " If you can't lick 'em, join 'em."

Yet the primary datum for both mass thought and elite thought alike is the extraordinary richness and complexity of reality, which I believe can always be trusted not to tolerate these artificial simplicities. Sophisticated thought delights in these false dilemmas. " Either the individual," it says, " or the society," whereas in fact the primary datum is the individual in society and society in the individual. " Either the material or the mental and spiritual," whereas immediate experience confronts us with all three not merely side by side but inextricably mingled with one another, so that to cognize the physical is a mental and spiritual experience and to enjoy mental and spiritual experience is at the same time a physical condition. Thus what we immediately experience is not merely the three and the absolute distinctions among them but their compresence in one world, even their complicity in one person or act. We live in a world in which almost every dilemma is false, a world in which every valid distinction separates, in thought, realities that can never be separated in fact. The result is a complexity and many-sidedness of reality which is an appalling intellectual burden for the philosopher and, in its own way, a terrible existential ordeal for the philosopher and nonphilosopher alike. Each has imposed upon him by reality the necessity of combining a physical, a mental, and a spiritual life within the unity of a single personal existence.

God has made the world too rich. In consequence the philosopher is intellectually frustrated and the common man continually out of his depth. It is not surprising that in this situation the philosopher resorts to a sophistication that promises to deliver him from his frustration, and the common man to a parallel brutalization of mass thought which at least gives him the illusion that his feet can touch the bottom of the pool as he splashes lazily in the shallows. The philosopher is continually at the end of his tether and his less gifted brethren feel again and again that they cannot bear so very much reality. Perhaps if men had made the world, they would have made a simpler, more streamlined job of it. Existence would have been less of a burden and thought, a more successful occupation. The trouble is that at the same time existence would have been more insipid and intellectual research less stimulating. Perhaps in a world in which everything is more or less easy nothing would have been worth-while. It is possible to utter even a human word on behalf of the divine point of view. We live a life in which nothing is simple, in the context of a world in which nothing is obvious. It is all very exhausting and all very exciting. The Christian at least would not have it otherwise.

Mass thought at its best, in its openness to experience, in its readiness for novelty and variety, provides a bracing challenge for elite thought. It is true to say that all the genuinely great philosophers of the Western tradition from Plato onward — as distinct from the many Sophists and minute philosophers with their artificial simplifications of reality — were attempting to respond to the challenge of mass thought and to provide us with philosophical apprehensions and reconstructions of reality which had all the breadth and comprehensive scope of mass thought, adding in the process, of course, a

rigor of rational articulation and a degree of critical, especially
self-critical, power which mass thought itself cannot pretend
to possess. In Plato and Aristotle, in the greater of the early
Christian fathers, in almost all the medievals, even in Descartes
and Spinoza, certainly in Leibnitz and Kant, in Locke (perhaps) and Berkeley (certainly) although not in Hume, even
again in Hegel and Whitehead, we encounter the same urge to
see life steadily and whole with an inclusive gaze that can
bring within the orbit of its vision and interpretation every
distinctive form of human experience and apprehension.

Mass thought not only permits but even positively invites
the elite refinement. Sophistication, on the other hand, frus-
trates mass thought and blinds the elites to its excellence. It is
sophistication that renders the elite thinker self-consciously
superior to the crudities of the irrational and superstitious mul-
titude. Yet this will not prevent him, as we have seen, from
accepting mass thought in its brutalized form. For many a contemporary elite thinker the brutalization of mass thought, its
disenchantment and secularization, is a sign of its progress.
From the standpoint of the positivist, for example, brutalized
mass thought is simply mass thought sufficiently educated to
agree rather crudely with his conclusions, only, of course, for
the wrong reasons. Such an observer sees only that brutalized
mass thought has lost its characteristic intellectual innocence,
its uncritical credulity. He fails to perceive that it has lost at
the same time its broad openness to experience, its sense of and
thirst for life in its manifold forms. The minute philosophers
relate themselves to mass thought at its weakest, just as the
great philosophers relate themselves to mass thought at its
broadest and best.

Sociologically speaking, we may perceive in these developments a clue to the widespread anti-intellectualism of the present time, the deep suspicion of our contemporary masses that
the elite thinkers do not do them justice and view their com-
mon-sense attitude toward life, with its wide-open receptivity
to experience, as a poor and unenlightened thing. To some ex-

tent, at all events, anti-intellectualism is a popular reaction against the sophistication of the elites. There is probably in the masses a widespread intuitive understanding that elite thought, in interpreting and grounding it, must necessarily go far beyond their apprehension of immediate experience. What they cannot understand or accept is that, in going beyond their immediate experience in order to interpret it, elite thought should somehow void it of its validity in the process. Hence, the popular mind suspects elite thought of a tendency to evade life and retreat from reality. It thinks of the philosopher as the inhabitant of an ivory tower. Worse still, as it contemplates its own brutalized elements, mass thought accuses elite thought, which has failed to appreciate and ignore its own authentic contribution, of perversely giving ideological support to its own most corrupted forms. It suspects, in other words, that sophisticated elite thought has failed to respond to the challenge of life to mind and hence is failing to fulfill its proper social function.

But if anti-intellectualism is caused by this chronic estrangement between the masses and the elites it also contributes to its intensification. The masses revolt against the elites because of their feeling that the elites cannot appreciate their open sensitivity, and the elites in turn revolt against the masses because it seems to them that the masses cannot appreciate their peculiar gifts and subtle contributions. And so the estrangement once begun moves rapidly from bad to worse. Left-wing, "tough" sophistication, which reaffirms mass thought in its brutalized form, is simply a desperate effort to overcome this chronic estrangement by improvising a new solidarity on the lowest possible level. Ecclesiastically speaking, the estrangement between the apologetic and the evangelistic ministry follows remarkably parallel lines. The evangelistic ministry addresses itself to mass thought in its most open and authentic form. It is profoundly in harmony with the orthodoxy of the classical Christian elites and indeed still evokes the elite articulations and critical refinements of their genuine successors. The apologetic ministry, on the other hand, is, above all, a ministry

to the sophisticated elites and apes the fashionable and prevalent forms of elite sophistication in generation after generation.
In the nineteenth century its general tendency was idealistic
and Hegelian, and the ghost of all this still survives, minus the
robust rationalism, of course, in a great deal of the so-called
Protestant neo-orthodoxy and in the obsession of so many theological elites, particularly in Germany and America, with existentialist thought. On the other hand, it is also true that in the
twentieth century the apologetic ministry finds itself compelled
to address those more or less positivistic elites who have re-
aligned themselves with mass thought in its brutalized forms.

Hence we find the same tendency to a drastically simplified
and reduced Christianity in the apologetic ministry as we find
in the elites to whom the ministry is addressed, a drastically
simplified and reduced metaphysic and philosophy of life.
Hence we find also in the churches the rise, since the Second
World War, of new movements of more or less fundamentalist
protest which reflect in theological terms the anti-intellectualism of the masses. Within the church we find the same problem
as confronts us in the world, a form of philosophical thought
and interpretation that is hopelessly out of touch with the mass
experience, a theologians' Christianity that is not the Christianity of the church as a whole, with the result that the real
Christianity that spiritually sustains the masses in the church
tends to go without theological articulation and intellectual
guidance. The trouble is, of course, that our churches support,
in the literal sense of providing and paying for them, both ministries at the same time, with the result that their intellectual
integrity is constantly threatened and compromised. Of course,
the same thing is true of society in general, which both accommodates the masses and employs the elites, so that the intellectual integrity of the church is just as much compromised as
the intellectual integrity of the civilization in which it finds itself, and to which it seeks to minister, and basically for the
same reasons.

In this book, of course, we are concerned primarily with the church. However, the solution of the problem within the church is very relevant to its solution within Western society as a whole, so that a contribution to the discussion on the theological level will also be a contribution, *mutatis mutandis*, to the parallel discussion on the secular level.

Chapter IV

The Critique of Liberalism:
(1) Its Use of History

Perhaps the most striking and significant difference between the classical Christianity common to the fathers, the Scholastics, and the Reformers, and self-consciously modern Christianity, as we have known it since the eighteenth century, has been found in their techniques of Biblical interpretation. We have already pointed out that the Bible interpreted in one way is almost a different book from the Bible interpreted in another. In one of his essays William Hazlitt recalls how he and Charles Lamb once took a Derbyshire schoolmaster named Burton, who was something of a mathematical prodigy, to see Edmund Keene play *Richard III*. At the end of the performance Burton knew how many words had been spoken during the play, calculated the cube root of this total to several places of decimals, and performed several other mathematical tricks of the same kind, but was quite unable to recollect either the plot or the theme of the drama. Physically Burton had undoubtedly been present at the performance, but it would be hard to claim that he had really seen or heard *Richard III*. What we may call the modern Bible, the Bible as it presents itself to modern man, differs in a similar way from the ancient Bible. It speaks to and evokes different interests, and the problem of interpreting it is handled in quite another way.

The aim of modern Biblical interpretation is to bring out its meaning by subjecting it to rigorous analysis in accordance with the dictates of historical methodology. This process of course includes, as always when the historical method uses written documents, a very close literary and philological analysis also.

The remote origins of this type of Biblical interpretation must no doubt be traced to the literary renaissance of the twelfth century, and in particular to the monks of the Abbey of St. Victor in Paris. Thomas Aquinas in the following century laid it down that the literal meaning of Scripture is the primary meaning, and that Scripture expounds nothing allegorically in one place which is not expressed literally in some other. On the other hand, it was still accepted that the allegorical interpretation of Scripture, though inferior to the literal, is valid and permissible. Broadly speaking, we may say that the attitude of the Reformers was more or less identical with that of Thomas. Modern historical methodology, particularly as applied to the Bible, begins in France at the end of the seventeenth century and develops considerably during the eighteenth century. In the nineteenth century occurred the great renaissance of historical studies in Germany, and it is primarily from this source that Protestant Christendom has been so tremendously influenced.

Of course, the development of historical methodology in the modern world has not been without philosophical repercussions and presuppositions. In Germany it was strongly influenced by Hegelian idealism. Elsewhere the chief influence has been a kind of naturalistic positivism, closely associated with the nominalism that first rose to dominance during the later Middle Ages. Hegelian idealism and nominalistic-naturalistic positivism differ sharply from each other; yet as far as the presuppositions of historical methodology are concerned they are perhaps more nearly akin than at any other point.[7] Naturalism after all, like idealism, is basically a form of monism. We may term it epistemological monism as distinct from ontological monism. For the Hegelians all is mind; for the naturalists all — or, if not all, at least all the knowable — is nature. These formulas differ in many important ways, but so far as historical methodology is concerned they come to very much the same thing. The nominalistic element in historical positivism would have us treat each particular historical episode on its own merits, in accordance with the particular evidences that have survived it. But the naturalistic development would insist on the basic presupposition that all episodes occur within the same continuum, that they have a kind of family resemblance to one another, so that none of them can contrast too sharply with the others. All historical events inhabit the same world; they belong to the same class or "real kind."

Whether naturalism is a form of pluralism or a form of monism is still a somewhat debatable point. We might perhaps describe it as a monism that indulges pluralistic moods. It would seem that if naturalism is taken to mean the doctrine that only nature (i.e., the subject matter of the natural sciences) exists, and that by the word "nature" we refer to a single broad continuum marked by recognizable uniformities and specific characteristics, then it is basically monistic. From this point of view history is a department of nature, characterized by the same ultimate uniformities, because it is part of the continuum which contains also the nonhistoric. Thus positivistic or nominalistic naturalism and absolute idealism converge from the point of view of historical methodology and historiography upon the same antisupernaturalistic conclusions, and it makes very little difference in practice which of these two philosophies the historian happens to prefer. If indeed there is something in history, or in certain episodes of history, to which such a uniform monism cannot do justice, then in relation to this particular element in history, or to these particular episodes, the modern historical method will be incapable of getting at the truth. Whether there is such an element in all history, or such episodes in history, is of course a philosophical and theological problem rather than a historical one, so that in the long run the question of historical methodology turns out to be a philosophical rather than a historical question. The historian can no more evade philosophy than the scientist or anyone else.

The philosophical affiliations of the ancient and early medieval Biblical commentators, however, were Platonic rather than idealistic or naturalistic. Often their methods were merely allegorical, in which case it made a great deal of difference whether, as in the case of Philo, they used Biblical episodes as allegories pointing to the truth of philosophical ideas external to the Bible and the Biblical tradition, or, as in the case of the orthodox Christian theologians, they interpreted Biblical events as allegorical expressions of theological ideas internal to the Bible and the Christian tradition. No doubt this is what Thomas Aquinas meant when he declared that the Bible contains nothing allegorical that is not expressed elsewhere in more literal fashion. In other words, orthodox allegorical interpretation did not give a free reign to the interpreter's imagination. On the contrary, it was strictly controlled by theology.

The modern reader of the patristic Biblical commentators, however, soon perceives that there is another method of Biblical interpretation which closely resembles allegory, and is easily mistaken for it, but which in fact expresses a quite different principle. This is what we nowadays call typology. There is something to be said for the view that the early Biblical commentators did not themselves notice the difference between typology and allegory. Once, however, the distinction has been observed it becomes for us a matter of first-rate importance. Typology notes analogous patterns of events and kindred themes which continually recur in the Bible, and for it Biblical interpretation is very largely an exposition of the meaning and content of these persistent and recurrent themes, which are, so to speak, " chronic " to the Bible. The moment we move over from the merely nominalistic notion that the Bible is a collection of many different books, accidentally bound together, to the notion that the Bible is one book that providentially collects and arranges its parts, we have to ask not merely the question, What does book Y or passage X mean in itself? but the much profounder question, What does book Y or passage X mean *in the Bible?* To be in the Bible is to be in a context that greatly modifies, perhaps even completely transforms, the meaning of that which is placed in the Bible.

A very clear, because extreme, instance is the question of the interpretation of the Song of Songs. Taken by itself, it is probably a collection of love poems or marriage songs, not unlike several other such collections emanating from the Middle East in the Hellenistic period which have also survived. Once, however, it has been incorporated in Scripture it can no longer merely mean what it manifestly means in itself, for now it has a new context. The interpretation of the Song of Songs in the Bible has tended to be either typological or allegorical. We can connect it with Hosea's notion of Israel as the bride of Yahweh and Paul's description of the church as the bride of Christ, or we can use it allegorically as an example of the kind of mysticism that delights to employ erotic images. The one thing we cannot do is to presume that the book means in the Bible precisely the same thing as it would have meant if it had never been included in the Bible, but had simply survived in some other way. To interpret it in the latter way, of course, would be genuine scholarly interpretation, but it would not be Biblical interpretation, for Biblical interpretation is always interpretation in context. The Bible modifies and qualifies its contents.

In the modern world we may say that the allegorical tradition of Philo and his Christian imitators is best represented by Bultmann and his followers, for they interpret Biblical episodes and events as images and symbols expressing a mode of philosophy external to the Biblical tradition, albeit in some ways and at some points responsive to at least a portion of that tradition. The typological method, on the other hand, is best represented today by Toynbee's famous *A Study of History*. One way of describing what Toynbee has tried to do, no doubt with only limited success, would be to say that he has attempted a typological interpretation of history, very similar to the typological Biblical interpretation that we find in early Biblical commentary. Thus we cannot say in the twentieth century that either allegorical or typological interpretation is a mere thing of the past incapable or unworthy of resurrection in our modern age.

As I have said, the philosophical affiliations of typology, which I take to be far more important than allegory, are primarily Platonic. The essential historical theme or pattern of events that recurs again and again in the course of history is a kind of Platonic universal, or " eternal object," to use the language of Whitehead, which is persistently ingredient to the course of history in an almost bewildering variety of particular exemplifications. To recognize the universal themes underlying these many variations is to be able to understand history, or, at least, to know what history is about. Thus typological interpretation, whether of Biblical history or of all history, aims at understanding as well as merely knowing what has happened. Of course, in Biblical interpretation there is always present the idea that the persistent underlying themes characterizing the Scriptures have achieved their perfect fulfillment and representation in Christ. One Platonic way of stating the doctrine of the incarnation would be to say that now at last the concrete universal has made itself particular, " for us men and for our salvation," and has thus become the clue to the interpretation of all particularities.

But there is a frankly religious as well as a philosophical reason for preferring, on the whole, ancient to modern Biblical commentary due to its manifestly greater theological and devotional effectiveness. Ancient Biblical commentary, though it was often childish and naïve, nevertheless at its best produced interpretations that were continuous with Scripture and possessed not a little of its literary grandeur and existential depth. Of modern Biblical commentary this could hardly be said, and on the few occasions when it is true, as for example in Sir Edwin C. Hoskyns and F. Noel Davey's *The Fourth Gospel*, we find to our surprise that most of the conventional Biblical scholars tend to be unimpressed and somewhat to decry and depreciate the book. This is not to say, of course, that the work of modern Biblical scholars is altogether worthless. By and large they have tended to find the kind of thing they were looking for. They have conscientiously endeavored, with some success, to fulfill the task of the historian as they understand it. It is their prevailing conception of the task of the historian that should be called in question. Their work has been dominated by some sort of nominalistic doctrine of external relations, so that usually they cannot see the difference between asking the question, What does passage X mean in itself? and asking the very different question, What does passage X mean in its context, that is, in the Bible? They have supposed that it is possible to investigate Biblical history without entering into questions of Biblical theology. It is, to say the least, doubtful whether this is in fact the case.

It was what we have called modernistic Christianity that was particularly influenced by positivistic, antisupernaturalistic historiography. According to this view, modern criticism has demonstrated that many, perhaps most, Biblical episodes cannot sustain the claim to historicity that has been made on their behalf. The suggestion, then, was that Christianity itself should be reduced to the theological interpretation of those Biblical events which are capable of withstanding this type of critique. This was the major theological problem of the first quarter or so of this present century. Now, however, we have moved — except here and there — from what we have called modernism to what we have called liberalism. The general tendency of liberalism is to accept the modernistic critique of the Scriptures but to claim that even those portions of the Bible which cannot withstand this critique may still be used and valued as religious myth; and that such a mental operation makes very little difference to Christianity, because the natural and appropriate language of religion is inherently mythic. Thus liberalism, unlike modernism, although accepting the same basic point of departure, can provide us with an unreduced Christianity. From this point of view it makes very little difference whether God speaks to us through symbolic events or through symbolic myths. Whether Biblical narratives are historical or mythical they still bear the same philosophical and religious meaning.

Of this point of view Bultmann is incomparably and justly the most famous representative. It is a point of view that reduces theology to something much more like speculative philosophy than science. It gets us away from empirical fact and from the possibility of testing ideas and hypotheses by reference to empirical fact. Of course, Bultmann differs from the early Christian allegorists, because his allegorical interpretation of Biblical events is controlled not by the central traditions of Christian theology but by existentialist philosophy, particularly in the form given to it by his phenomenologist colleague, Martin Heidegger. Nevertheless, the method in general resembles that of the allegorists.

Of course we have to consider the question whether in fact the proper and appropriate language of religious expression is mythic. Certainly we can find myths in the Bible, and no doubt the various Mediterranean and Middle Eastern polytheistic paganisms, which form the ultimate context of the Scriptures, were entirely or almost wholly mythic. Nevertheless Christianity, and for that matter the Hebraic religion of the Old Testament, always claimed to distinguish itself from polytheistic paganism precisely on this account. This is certainly true when we come to the early Christian missions among the Gentiles. Even if we were to allow that the natural and appropriate language of religion is mythic, we should still have to consider the question, In what sense is Christianity to be regarded as a religion at all?

For the distinction between Christianity and religion is of great importance in contemporary discussion. Religion, after all, is basically a human activity, although in many cases we must call it a heroic and inspired one. Apparently every human culture pattern, however primitive, includes a religious element. Wherever we find men we find some sort of religion going on. But the basic category of Christianity is not the concept of what we may call " the religious " in man, demanding and

receiving expression, but rather the concept of revelation.
From this point of view we may be inclined to say Christianity
is not *a* religion but *the* gospel, or, perhaps better, because this
formula does justice to the obvious kinship between Christianity and the religions, Christianity is the redemption of religion, the transubstantiation of religion from being the embodi-
ment and expression of man's natural religious propensities
into something that organically re-relates him to God. Or, to
put it in still another way, religion is a human activity, Christianity a divine activity. It is not, of course, that men are inactive
in Christianity, but rather that Christianity insists that the ter-
restrial actions of Christians are all of them more or less adequate, or more or less inadequate, responses to a divine initiative.

Now it may very well be argued that mythology, which at its
best may be very adequate for the expression of the human religious consciousness, is quite incapable of making manifest the
divine initiative. Mythology might express the general idea that
God *could* do something; what it could never do is make manifest the reality of God actually doing something, and there is
a vast difference between the mere idea that God might or
could do something and the emphatic assertion that he has in
fact done a specific something. Nowadays we hear a good deal
from contemporary theologians about the difference between
the dynamic, living God of the Bible, and what is usually described and dismissed as the static, or inert, "dead God" of
Greek philosophy. No doubt this distinction is too sharp and
clearly articulated to do justice either to the depths of God in
the Bible or to the very real activity ascribed to God in
Greek philosophy, but that is not the point in mentioning the
distinction here. What must be emphasized here is that the
mere idea of an active God who does something is quite as
static as the mere idea of a static God who does nothing. Ideas
are meant to be static, for intelligible discussion would otherwise be impossible. The Bible does not merely present the
idea of a God who acts; rather, it presents us with the concrete

evidence and reality of God's acting.

Thus the Bible does not expound to us the philosophical and speculative idea of the living God; rather, it makes manifest the divine acts. If we transform the Biblical narratives that testify to the divine action into symbolic myths, we shall not be expressing the Biblical idea of the living God in a new way; rather, we shall be abolishing the evidence upon which that assertion rested.

The truth is that it is not only myths that are symbolical. We live in a universe in which facts and events are symbolic also. For the psalmist the heavens declare the glory of God, and for the Old Testament prophets the historical events that enter into the experience of Israel symbolize and expound the judgment, the purpose, and the mercy of God. Indeed, it is in the Hebrew prophets that we pass, through a withering criticism of mythology, to the view that history is the proper locus of revelation.

What we often call the "real world of our experience," it might perhaps be better to call "our empirical world," for to call the world of our experience the "real world" is, after all, to beg a rather large philosophical question. For myself I think the world of our experience is real — using the word "real" analogically — but I doubt very much whether we are justified in calling it *the* real world. I should, however, reject the view that our empirical world is an unreal world of appearance only. The main point for us here is that our empirical world is a realm of symbolism. It consists exclusively of signs and things signified which are not capable of functioning as signs, the things with which we are concerned in metaphysics.

Any empirically real thing, whether object, event, or enduring process, consists, in our experience of it, of that which symbolizes it plus that which it symbolizes. We cannot distinguish absolutely between that which is symbolized and that which symbolizes it because in our empirical world an item of experience is not recognized as such until, however inadequately, it has been symbolized; and it does not become truly

meaningful for us until we have some idea, again however inadequate, of what it symbolizes. The basis of this philosophical
understanding of symbolism is thus an outright rejection of any
notion of any kind of dualism between an objective reality that
is symbolized and a proximate system of man-made conven-
tions that symbolize it. On the contrary, reality lends itself to
symbolism and can only be grasped in symbols precisely because reality itself is intrinsically symbolic. To sum up: in our
empirical world to enter into the realm of significant experience
is to be symbolized, and to be symbolized is to be known and
recognized as a possible symbol. Our world is a world of symbols, and the symbolic world is the real world, in so far as we
may correctly speak of our world as real.

Our most important as well as our most highly elaborated
system of symbols is language. But we mistake the nature of
language if we regard it merely or even primarily as a means
of communication. On the contrary, language is that which
makes significant experience possible. It is in terms of language that we both experience and think about the empirical
world in which we find ourselves. For us to experience anything is to name it, or, if we cannot name it, to utter a confus-
ing, because confused, description of it, which declares it to be
like and yet unlike something else and complains of the intellectual frustration to which we are subjected by the absence
of a name. Of course we cannot convert this proposition. If to
experience anything is to name it, it by no means follows that
to name anything is necessarily to experience it.

But the primary importance of verbal symbols in the world
of our experience and in the realm of our discussion must not
obscure the fact that the realities to which our verbal symbols
refer are themselves symbolic. It is true that the symbolic character of the realities to which our verbal symbols refer can only
be observed, experienced, and expounded in terms of further
verbal symbols. Thus we may say that the clouds are dark and
heavy — that is to symbolize the present reality with verbal
symbols; we may then add that this means that it will rain very

shortly — that is to symbolize what the reality symbolizes with fresh verbal symbols. Yet in this latter case what the verbal symbols are symbolizing is the symbolic character or import of that which the first set of verbal symbols symbolizes.

Thus there is a real as well as a verbal symbolism even though we may require verbal symbols in order to experience and report what the real symbol symbolizes. This distinction between the real symbol and the verbal symbol is important, and I lay some stress upon it precisely because the very fact that real symbolism is only known to us and reported to us in terms of verbal symbolism might easily mislead us into a failure to observe the difference between real symbolism and verbal symbolism. It is because the realities that verbal symbolism enables us to observe and report are themselves symbolic that it is possible for us adequately to symbolize them. Thus we escape from the error of supposing that a reality which is non-symbolic in its own nature can nevertheless be adequately known and reported in symbolic terms. On the contrary, to enter more and more deeply into the nature of the reality to which our symbols refer is to lay bare more and more insightfully its own intrinsically symbolic character. To know what our signs signify is to recognize in turn what the reality signifies.

Of course, although the roots of symbolism are to be found in reality rather than in human convention, it is also true that men can and do create symbols. Living in the symbolic world creates and fosters our ability to do so. Merely conventional symbols can be devised by individual persons, but more often and more importantly in human history they are created and conserved by societies rather than by individual persons. It is well known that we are living through a time of profound historical change and social crisis in which men find it more and more difficult to enter into the symbolic inheritance characteristic of the societies to which they belong. This has sometimes been called the " disenchantment of modern man." But this disenchantment does not mean that modern man has ceased to require or is no longer able to use symbols. It simply means that on account of his estrangement from the traditional social symbols he is more and more compelled to devise new systems of symbolism for himself. The result of this is a chaos of systems of personal symbolism which are unintelligible in whole societies and only meaningful in and for small cliques. We see this in the frustration of what has long been called "contemporary" art. After several centuries of romantic naturalism and sensualism in art we are now returning to a more intellectualized art. Since we no longer have any common apparatus of symbols in terms of which our artists can work, for most people contemporary art looks like a series of occult essays in the unintelligible.

Christian evangelism finds itself in a somewhat similar predicament, for the symbolic language in terms of which Christianity has for so long affirmed itself and explored its own meaning is also one from which contemporary society is estranged. For the evangelist to invent a new language for his purpose is to condemn himself to frustrations analogous to those of the contemporary artists. At best his language will become the language of a clique, and almost certainly never that of a whole society. I remember hearing an English bishop remark that there could be no general return to Christianity without a parallel revival of the habit of poetry reading. This appealed to me as a percipient observation pointing to the very roots of our Christian concern for what are usually called the humanities.

The resurrection of the gospel must necessarily be preceded by the resurrection of its proper language. The Christian attitude in the modern world is inevitably, it would seem to me, accompanied by a kind of cultural conservatism, which must be absolutely distinguished from any kind of political or economic conservatism. The cultural conservatism is concerned to conserve a culture, whereas contemporary political and economic conservatisms are attempting to conserve precisely those political and economic processes and institutions which have slowly but relentlessly estranged the mass of mankind from that culture. Thus the cultural conservatism can never be reconciled with, and must remain antithetical to, the political and economic conservatism with which it is sometimes so mistakenly and inharmoniously mated. Nor is this cultural conservatism in any sense backward-looking or reactionary. It is essentially a struggle to preserve a language and an apparatus of symbolic forms in terms of which new things can be said, and it fights against the danger of a semantic chaos in terms of which nothing, whether new or old, can intelligibly be said at all.

Paradoxically enough, we can only say new things in a world in which men go on saying old things, for to assert the old things is not merely to reassert them but also to keep alive the language in terms of which the new things can intelligibly be said. Thus a concern for the longevity of symbolic forms is an attitude at the same time conservative and progressive. Indifference to the longevity of the symbolic form, by cutting us off from our roots in the past, destroys our capacity to grow in the future. This digression is important because it indicates the historical and even political relevance of the contemporary philosophical concern with the problems of symbolism.

The symbolic character of all experience, and of the world of our experience, reminds us of the symbolic character of all knowledge, and this in its turn makes us aware of the aesthetic character of knowledge. The quest for knowledge is always and necessarily a quest for more and more appropriate symbols, and the capacity to recognize the apparent or real fittingness of a symbol necessarily includes an element analogous to that which in aesthetics is usually called " taste." The idea of an aesthetic element in knowledge has in the past usually been emphasized in the area of the philosophy of science, particularly in connection with the elegance and rational beauty of mathematical demonstrations. In this sense it goes back at least as far as Copernicus. I would wish to go far beyond this and locate the aesthetic element in knowledge particularly in the realms of theology and metaphysics, where, above all, we are concerned with the appropriateness and adequacy of analogies.

The metaphysician is primarily concerned with the selection of *fitting* symbols, and with the interpretation of the symbolic import of that which these fitting symbols symbolize.

The philosopher and the theologian are related to the spectacle of life as a whole very much as the dramatic critic is related to the drama. The best kind of dramatic criticism is not simply a nonliterary intellectualism about literature. It inhabits the world which it interprets. There is always something suspect about literary criticism that is not literature, and alas, so much contemporary criticism is so manifestly not literature. To interpret drama is not merely to analyze its structure or specify its method but to unfold its meaning, and the meaning of drama is itself a dramatic event. It may well be necessary for the critic to analyze the structure of the drama and to determine and characterize the method by which it unfolds its meaning, but such activities are not ends in themselves; rather, they are instrumental to the primary purpose of the dramatic criticism, which is always to unfold the meaning of the drama. Because the world of our experience is a symbolic world, it is a dramatic world, so that its meaning can only be unfolded dramatically. In such a world, to know is to know the meaning of symbolism, and the quest for such a knowledge is necessarily an aesthetic one.

All this makes it clear why it is that myth-symbols have played such an important role in the development of philosophical and theological knowledge. Truth cannot be told without myth because reality is drama rather than process. In the language that we have been employing we may distinguish between drama and process by saying that, whereas in the language in which we unfold the meaning of drama we are using symbols to refer to a reality that is in itself symbolic, in the case of process we use our symbols to analyze a reality whose symbolic character is systematically ignored. The language that analyzes and defines the process is itself meaningful, in the sense of pointing beyond itself to the process, but the process defined has not, as thus defined, the same visibly symbolic character. But the language that unfolds the meaning of the drama points to a reality that, like itself, is symbolic. Hence the superiority of mythical language in all those intellectual quests in which we are seeking an ultimate truth, in the sense of an intellectual continuity with the inherent character of ultimate reality.

Mythical language, even when the content of the myth, historically speaking, is quite untrue, is always saying to us in effect, " It was like this, or something of the kind." It is when myth says, " or something of the kind," that it clearly implies its dramatic understanding of reality. It may not in fact have been quite like this, but the reality was certainly something of the same dramatic kind. Process language, by contrast, says to us in effect, " This is the way in which it worked, and yet it wasn't really like this at all; for the reality was a dramatic event, whereas all we can observe in this particular way and chronicle in this particular language is a process."

It is here also that we must observe the relevance of the doctrine of the ultimate singularity of reality, or, better, of the singularity of the ultimate reality. The life of the singular is drama and we can have no insight into its meaning unless we diagnose and interpret it as drama. Here we must distinguish carefully between the terms *a* singular and *the* singular. As conventionally used in contemporary logical discussion, the term "*a* singular " usually means little more than any particular particular. To talk about *a* singular is almost invariably the prelude to ignoring its singularity, as indeed for many scientific and other purposes we must ignore its singularity. But the term "*the* singular" always refers to that absolute singular which is necessarily *entirely* ignored whenever its singularity is ignored. For us, of course, *the* singular in this absolute sense is God. Hence the only adequate language in terms of which we can refer to ultimate reality is dramatic language, which restricts both theology and metaphysics to the language of myth-symbols and event-symbols, although they may, of course, employ another, more analytic and definitive language when subsequently meditating upon their primary symbols.

All this indicates the impossibility of either a demythologized metaphysics or a demythologized theology or a demythologized preaching of the gospel. We may exclude certain particular myths on aesthetic-intellectual grounds, but a totally demythologized account of our world is necessarily a false and misleading account. Loyalty to truth itself demands of us the resort to mythological language. Particularly misleading is the supposition by some contemporary theologians that we can substitute for a mythological account of the world in which we are an existentialist account of that existence which we have in this world. In fact the dramatic-existentialist account of the existence which we have in this world becomes incredible and makes no sense if we insist on giving a radically demythologized account of the world in which we exist. The hiatus between our dramatic-existentialist account of man and a purely process-scientific account of the world in which he finds himself is too great for the intellect to tolerate. It is another form of that prevalent but fatal tendency to concede the physical universe to science while reserving man and man alone as the proper and exclusive province of philosophy and theology.

This is an impossible way of dividing the spoils. Science will insist, and rightly, on treating man and human existence in its own nondramatic, process terms; theology and philosophy must persist in treating even the physical universe in its own dramatic, mythological language. Only so can we come to any clear awareness of the fact that there is no more an inherent conflict between these two languages than there is between, shall we say, English and French. The more clearly we see the difference between theology, on the one hand, and natural science, on the other, as a semantic difference, the more rapidly we shall be rescued from the fatal notion that there is any necessary and essential conflict between science and Christian belief. The existentialist account of human existence only makes sense against the background provided by a mythological account of the world's existence.

But although the myth-symbol thus rests upon and keeps us aware of an important theological and metaphysical truth, preserving our sense of the inherently dramatic character of reality, it has at the same time very severe and cramping limitations from the point of view of both theology and metaphysics. Myth successfully indicates the dramatic character of reality, but it can never with any certainty specify the drama. It is related to the drama of reality rather like those imaginary epical histories which some gifted children, e.g., the Brontës and C. S. Lewis, have been known to compose at great length. It leaves us saying that although this is certainly the *kind of thing* of which reality is composed, yet to be aware of the *kind of thing* of which the ultimate truth is composed is nevertheless not to be aware of the ultimate truth. The ultimate truth, if we knew it, would be more like myth than like the theories in which we so successfully analyze processes, but that does not mean that it would necessarily be like any particular myth. It is one thing to say that the ultimate truth must resemble myth in the literary and expressive form of that which adequately symbolizes it; it is quite another thing to say that some particular myth is true.

Myth is at its best when it indicates in its own characteristic way some kind of existential generality — if the rather paradoxical phrase " existential generality " may be permitted. Myth, in other words, is at its best when it endeavors to interpret and express something universal in human condition. In this context it is superior to any kind of psychological or anthropological theory. Pure theory, however useful, ultimately fails as a mode of apprehending and declaring the truth about the human condition because it is incapable of grasping and communicating the fact that the human condition is always and necessarily dramatic in character. Theory can only analyze process; it cannot describe or re-create drama. Thus the story of Adam's fall and exclusion from the Garden of Eden and subsequent career as an agriculturalist can be duplicated in terms of pure anthropological theory. The desiccation of the soil of a

large area in the Middle East primitively inhabited by simple
food gatherers confronted them with a situation in which they
could either die of starvation, or migrate to the more fertile
area farther south, or respond to the challenge of these more
intimidating conditions by practicing very simple agricultural
techniques. No doubt many, perhaps most, died of starvation;
others migrated to the south; but a few like Adam became agricultural laborers. As theory describes it, the whole episode is
seen as a process. But in the case of each of the individual
agents concerned, it was not a process but a drama, and in this
sense the Adam story is much closer to the actual historical
truth — not, of course, in factual detail but in existential form.

So far as metaphysics and theology are concerned, however,
myth only tells us that the truth, if we were to possess it, would
be more akin to myth than to theory. It cannot tell us what the
truth is. Thus the function of the myth-symbol is to convey primary and universal existential truth. Perhaps one of the most
successful and typical of all myths is the story of the tempta-
tion of Eve in the garden. The insight into the nature of sinful-
ness is of a radical and profound character. It is still true to
this day that the best way of embarking on an exposition of the
nature of sin is to shape it as a commentary on the meaning of
this tense existential drama, very much as a dramatic critic
may comment on the meaning of a stage play.

We may note that nothing is added to the meaning or the
force of a genuine myth by attributing historicity to it. People
often attribute historicity to myths, but the meaning of the
myth remains unchanged whether we attribute historicity to it
or not. Whether Eve was a historical personage or not is quite
irrelevant to the point and power of the story. It is possible to
regard her as a historical personage yet to miss the essential
import of the narrative. Conversely, those who deny to Eve
any historical existence may nevertheless perceive and learn
from the myth all that the myth has to teach. The moral of this
seems to be that even when we do sometimes, perhaps correctly, attribute historicity to our myths, we must always re-

gard this attribute of historicity as quite accidental and ignore it in practice. The upshot is clear, the primary reference of the myth is always human and existential. It can never really encompass the metaphysical and theological singular. We can build no metaphysical or theological proclamation upon myth, apart from the observation that metaphysical and theological truth, if it were to come into our possession, would resemble myth rather than theory. For metaphysical and theological truth is necessarily truth about the existence and behavior of the ultimate singular, dramatic in its inherent character, and therefore demanding drama as the intellectual mode in which it is grasped and communicated.

What we have already said about the way in which many myth-symbols may, rightly or wrongly, have historicity attributed to them, but always accidentally and quite irrelevantly to their meaning, may have prepared for us the observation that many event-symbols function primarily as myth-symbols. Thus, for example, the career of Napoleon may symbolize for us what Toynbee calls " the nemesis of militarism." The story of Napoleon would do this for us even if Napoleon had never existed. From the point of view of its central symbolic function the fact that Napoleon actually existed neither adds to nor detracts from the symbolic adequacy of the Napoleonic myth. Thus many, perhaps most, event-symbols do not differ significantly from myth-symbols. On the other hand, it is certainly true — and this is quite vital to the whole character of Christianity — that some event-symbols do appear, to the minds of those who enter profoundly into their meaning, to achieve a metaphysical and theological reference that we have seen to be beyond the capacity of the myth-symbol. This occurs when certain events are taken to be self-revelatory acts of the living God. In this case they symbolize not something universal in the human condition but something specific and proper to the divine or singular existence. In the case of these symbols historicity is not irrelevant to their symbolic function. True event symbols must *occur* in order to symbolize whatever it is that they symbolize. Thus to translate such event-symbols into myth-symbols is to transpose altogether the direction of their symbolic reference.

Let us take as examples the two New Testament miracles par excellence that predominate over all the others, and that create for the contemporary mind, whether Christian or not, the problem of miracle in its most acute form — the virgin birth and the empty tomb. Some contemporary Christian apologists and theologians have in effect proposed that we should treat these two narratives as myth-symbols rather than event-symbols, and affirm their symbolic meaning while denying their historical occurrence. No doubt they are encouraged in this course by the complete success with which contemporary Christianity has done this in the case of what are very obviously pure myth-symbols. Thus the fundamentalists have insisted on attributing historicity to the Garden of Eden myth. We have found that nothing is lost by denying the historicity while continuing to affirm the symbolic content. This is because, even when historicity was attributed to it, the Garden of Eden story was always a myth-symbol and never an event-symbol. It does not therefore follow that the same intellectual stratagem can be pursued with equal success when we have to do with genuine event-symbols, which from the very beginning were received and interpreted as event-symbols, so that the attribution to them of a mythical character involves imposing upon them a novel interpretation that has never been their function in the traditional world of meaning to which they belong.

Obviously we could make the legendary story function as a myth. If the virgin birth story is a myth, it symbolizes something universal in the human condition. Treated in this way the most obvious meaning of the virgin birth story is a radical incompatibility between sexuality and spirituality. This is in fact the way in which the virgin birth narrative has been interpreted by those sinister Manichaean influences which have sometimes opposed Christianity from without and at other times infiltrated it from within. It must be confessed that if the virgin birth narrative is to be treated as a myth-symbol this is the most obvious and persuasive way of interpreting its symbolic content. The trouble is that this method of interpreting the narrative attributes to it a meaning that the orthodox Christian must necessarily deny.

But in orthodox Christianity, and considered from its place in the Biblical tradition, the virgin birth narrative is not and never has been a myth-symbol. On the contrary, it is an event-symbol with a quite specific reference of an utterly singular character. Considered as an event-symbol its meaning is plain: the incarnate Son of God, by the will of the Father and through the power of the Holy Ghost, *enters into* the world process and does not *emerge out of* it. To use another, equally contemporary, language, the incarnation is not the apex of an evolutionary process but an entirely novel act of God akin in its character to the creation itself. Hence, the use of the title " Second Adam " in relation to the incarnate Son of God. But for the event-symbol to possess this singular symbolic content it must occur. The virgin birth narrative treated as a myth-symbol does not and cannot possess the same symbolic content. When we treat the virgin birth narrative as an event-symbol, with this singular metaphysical and theological symbolic reference, what we are interested in is not anything that the *story* of the virgin birth reveals but what the *fact* of the virgin birth reveals. The fact of the virgin birth indicates a paradoxical continuity that is as much a discontinuity as a continuity: a new beginning for humanity and at the same time a continuation of the human race.

The essential point is metaphysically and theologically grounded, and therefore clarified, when we recollect that the act of the living God, who is both transcendent and immanent, must always be characterized by both an immanent aspect (continuity) and a transcendent aspect (discontinuity). The divine activity characteristically brings out of the given, the existent, things both new and old. It sustains and continues

the creation at the same time as it renews it. Thus we may
say that the basic pattern of the virgin birth is at one with the
basic pattern of all divine action.

We might even reflect upon the relationship of this paradox
of the discontinuous continuity to the interpretation of the
meaning of evolution, perhaps even to that of the principle of
indeterminacy in quantum physics. Certainly we can perceive
the same pattern also in the novelties and originalities that
emerge in the course of human social and cultural development. Moments of originality in the arts, the sciences, and
philosophy are always at the same time both continuous and
discontinuous with the traditions out of which they emerge.
Beethoven, for example, is inconceivable apart from the development of German music during the eighteenth century. That
development prepared for him both the classical forms in
terms of which he thought and the technical means that he
employed, the symphony orchestra. Yet if Beethoven was
manifestly *out of* the tradition as he found it, it is equally plain
that he was not *by* it, that he was a discontinuity as much as a
continuity. We can observe precisely the same motifs in Darwin and Einstein, in Kant and Thomas Aquinas. If we may
continue to borrow the language of the stud farm, we may say
that mere developments are both *by* and *out of* the tradition,
but that genuine novelties are always *out of* the tradition but
not *by* it. Thus we may say that the basic pattern of divine
action in the virgin birth is characteristically the pattern of
all divine action whatsoever, and of all that human action
which approximates to greatness and creativity. In this generalized sense the pattern disclosed in virginal conception and
birth is one of which human experience continually reminds
us, and to which the human race is more heavily indebted than
to perhaps any other of the creative ways of God, in whose
image we are made.

Thus it is only when regarded as an event-symbol that the
virgin birth is capable of bearing a Christian meaning. If I
were to regard it as a myth-symbol, I should feel, as a Chris-

tian, compelled to reject it as a thoroughly inadequate and misleading one. The apologetic problem still, of course, remains. For the virgin birth, if it actually happened, was a miracle, but of that I shall say nothing here. I am simply concerned for the moment with the purely negative conclusion that the device of treating the virgin birth narrative as a myth is completely unsatisfactory from the point of view of Christian thought, and offers no hope of any solution of the apologetic problem.

In many ways the resurrection narrative and proclamation, taken as including the empty tomb motif, make this distinction even more overwhelmingly clear. Some writers distinguish between the resurrection narrative and the empty tomb motif, but there is a better warrant for considering the whole body of testimony in its unity. It is true, of course, that, as some point out, the empty tomb does not prove the resurrection, but that is not the question. A more relevant way of stating the question would be to ask whether a full tomb would not disprove the resurrection. Again, perhaps a reply could be given in the negative, but at least the assertion that the tomb was occupied in the usual way would entirely alter our idea of what the resurrection was.

Given a full tomb, the resurrection becomes an example of the kind of thing that provides the theme of "spiritualist" discourses rather than of Christian theology. It takes us into a world of astral bodies, materializations, and hitherto undreamed of dimensions, and out of the world of positive realism and direct testimony which we find in the New Testament. The apostles and the early Christians, one may feel, were hardly capable of such subtleties and sophistications as these. Whatever the resurrection testimony meant to them it cannot have meant anything like or even continuous with what the modern theologian has in mind when with one breath he asserts the resurrection and then denies the empty tomb with the next. Of course the testimony itself insists primarily upon the appearances and relegates the empty tomb comparatively to the background, just as, if I meet my friend by chance at the opera, I should normally, and under most circumstances, say that I met him at the opera rather than that I knew he was not home because I met him at the opera. Nevertheless, there is good ground for taking the empty tomb story as an integral part of the resurrection narrative rather than as a mere addition to it. At least we must grant to those who deny the empty tomb that the resurrection event cannot mean or symbolize that which it means and symbolizes in the historic Christian tradition.

This is brought out very clearly, and quite unintentionally, by Basil Willey in his thoughtful and reverent little book *Christianity, Past and Present:*

> Try as I may, I cannot bring myself to feel that my religion ought to stand or fall by the historical accuracy of such a story as this (i.e., the resurrection). . . . If I really knew that it happened, or that any other miracle happened — if it could be demonstrated to me, then I should have to accept it, and it would no longer be a truth of faith. As long as it remains a truth of faith it can mean "I hold by faith, that the sovereignty of God triumphs over the ambiguous course of history, and I hope, through repentance, that that faith may be kept real in me." [8]

This passage will repay careful analysis. In the first place the apostolic witness to the resurrection is not put forward primarily as a truth of faith. Christian faith is not the faith that something or other happened but faith in the sense of trust and hope in God. Even those who speak of their faith in the resurrection really mean, not so much a faith in the resurrection considered as an event, but their faith in the honesty and trustworthiness of the apostolic testimony to the resurrection. In the New Testament witness the resurrection is a public event of which the witnesses bear their testimony. "This was not done in a corner." (Acts 26:26, RSV.) It is a mighty act or sign of God which evokes and sustains faith. We do not believe in the resurrection event because we have Christian faith; rather, we have Christian faith because we believe in the resurrection event. In other words, the New Testament testimony to the resurrection is not a faith-truth but a historical truth, a historical truth that arouses, or even causes, faith in the minds of those who find themselves confronted by it, who in the depths of themselves know that they cannot honestly evade the testimony.

The modern conception that revelation takes place primarily through events — no more, after all, than a return to the Biblical conception — implies that events precede and cause faith, and that the events which provoke and sustain faith are not themselves the product of faith. In other words, this conception of revelation implies that historical truth precedes faith — truth both in logic and in time: first the event, then the faith which it arouses as the inevitable response to its factuality. But this faith is not the faith that the event happened; rather, it is a faith in God, in the righteousness and steadfastness of his purpose, by whom and through whom the event was brought about and of whom the event is a sign. Thus the resurrection is, properly speaking, a truth of faith only in a secondary sense for all those postapostolic Christians who did not witness it but accepted instead the testimony of the original witnesses.

But even more interesting is the meaning that Willey attributes to the resurrection narrative interpreted as a myth-symbol. " I hold, by faith, that the sovereignty of God triumphs over the ambiguous course of history, and I hope, through repentance, that that faith may be kept real in me." No doubt this is the best that can be done with the resurrection narrative once we agree to treat it as a myth-symbol, and it must be admitted that even this is something, but it is very much less than the unique and singular meaning attributed to the resurrection narrative in the apostolic witness. " Let all the house of Israel therefore know assuredly that God has made him both Lord and Christ, this Jesus whom you crucified." (Acts 2:36, RSV.) It is a far cry from Peter to Basil Willey. Yet the difference is quite explicable in terms of the concepts that have been elaborated in this chapter. For the apostle the resurrection narrative is an event-symbol that reveals the one living God in action, not a myth-symbol suggesting in vivid and moving terms a generality that warrants an optimistic view about the ultimacies of the human condition. We may perhaps feel compelled, nevertheless, to take sides with Basil Willey rather than with The Acts of the Apostles, but do not let us suppose that we can transmute the event-symbol into a myth-symbol without entirely altering its meaning. Again the apologetic question still remains and of that deliberately I say nothing here, because it would take us beyond the limits of the present discussion.

We may perhaps sum up the whole trend of this prolonged contrasting of myth-symbolism with event-symbolism in a single sentence. *Man made religion, which is therefore mythic, but God gave the gospel, which is therefore eventual or historic.*

Myth at its best is existential and insightful, but only events are theologically revealing. Myth can convey and express human ideas — and primarily, human ideas about the human; but only from the event — that is, in and through the divine activity — can be derived any knowledge of the God who is and acts, the living God who presents himself to us in the Biblical testimony.

To say all this perhaps raises for us in an acute form the problem of faith. We are familiar enough, of course, with the old faith-versus-reason controversy, which so dominated religious and apologetic writing during the eighteenth century. It has less often been noticed that the eighteenth century also indulged in a parallel controversy, that between the English empiricists and the European rationalists, which might very well be described as a perception-versus-reason controversy. The two discussions leave us with three primary modes of cognition: sense perception, conceptual reason, and spiritual faith. Yet there must be a fundamental error in the notion of some kind of antithesis between any two of these three. Human perception is not prior to reason; it is an operation carried on by a rational or intellectual being. We human beings only know perception within the context of rationality. Similarly, as Richard Hooker pointed out, human faith is always the faith of rational beings, otherwise the word of God might equally well have been proclaimed to animals.[9] We err if we restrict reason to the mere handling of concepts. Man is as rational in perception and faith as in conception. We must distinguish between these three activities, but not in such a fashion as to divide and oppose them. The particular form of this type of controversy which we have raised in this chapter, however, is the less familiar one of faith and history. What are we to say when faith compels us to affirm the historicity of events which, from the point of view of the historians' careful investigation of the extant evidences, must be pronounced at least "not proven"?

It must be observed that there is not a specific kind of faith-truth to be absolutely distinguished from philosophical or historical truth. The things that faith affirms have the same modality as the things that philosophy or history may affirm. In faith it is the ground, reason, and motive that persuade us to make the affirmation, rather than its content, which is to be distinguished from philosophy and history. Christian affirmations are sometimes metaphysical and sometimes historical. Christian metaphysical affirmations differ from ordinary metaphysical propositions because they are not merely the product of speculative metaphysical reasoning — but not in any other way. Similarly, Christian historical affirmations differ from ordinary historical affirmations because they are not merely the product of a critical investigation of extant evidences, but otherwise they do not differ. A metaphysical proposition is a proposition about metaphysics, but not necessarily a proposition derived from metaphysical reasoning. Similarly, a historical proposition is a proposition about history, but not necessarily a proposition derived from a prolonged course of historical research.

When we say that Christianity is a historical religion we certainly do not mean that it is the historian's religion, for not all Christians are historians, nor are all historians Christians. Nor do we mean that Christianity is a doctrine in which theological truth must constantly wait upon the verdicts of historical research. On the contrary, when we say that Christianity is *the* historical religion we mean that it is characteristically the religion that compels men to make historical affirmations on the ground of faith. In other words, it is not that the religion depends on the history but rather that the history depends on the religion. A historical hypothesis, such as that theological hypothesis by means of which the Christian thinker orders and makes sense of the New Testament data, is not, of course, in this particular case a purely historical hypothesis. It contains metaphysical and theological elements. It depends heavily, for instance, on the doctrine of the Trinity. There is in the Godhead that which is eternally Father and that which is eternally Son. He who is eternally Son was made man in the womb of the Virgin Mary, lived a totally human life, and died an excruciating human death for our salvation. It is important to note that the Son of God did not become the Son merely by the act of the incarnation. That is an elementary Christological mistake which is unfortunately rather prevalent at the present time.

There is thus an eternal Son of God who became man in the incarnation. This human life, nature, and career which the Son of God took and made his own in the incarnation is called Jesus of Nazareth. The doctrine of the incarnation does not mean that God had a special relationship with a man called Jesus of Nazareth. Rather, it means that in and through Jesus of Nazareth, God has a new and special relationship to the entire human race. Again, the relationship is not the consequence or upshot of the special union of the divine and the human disclosed in the actual moral and spiritual life of Jesus of Nazareth. On the contrary, the union of the human with the divine which we find in the actual historical career of Jesus of Nazareth is the upshot and consequence of the underlying metaphysical event of the incarnation.

Clearly we cannot expect that historical research could in any way demonstrate that this Christian hypothesis must be true. If it is true, of course, it is true in history, but that does not mean that it is true of history or merely for the historian. History deals with phenomena, whereas Christian doctrine deals with noumena, with the ground and interpretation of the phenomena. The theological interpretation of the New Testament data is metaphysical; or, perhaps a better word in this particular context would be "metahistorical." A metahistorical hypothesis can no more be demonstrated by historical research than a metaphysical hypothesis can be demonstrated by physics. On the other hand, it can to some extent be verified in terms of history. Although the historical facts cannot demonstrate the hypothesis, they must at least be compatible with it; and we must find in the hypothesis a principle of interpretation in terms of which we can grasp and articulate the meaning of the phenomena.

The main task of the church's theology, from this point of view, is to give meaning to the New Testament. Although we can trace a real beginning of this theological task in the epistles of Paul and elsewhere in the New Testament, we must say that considered as a whole the New Testament, like any other historical record and testimony, fails to give meaning to itself. Thus we notice that wherever and whenever men have endeavored to interpret the New Testament without or apart from theology, the consequence is intellectual chaos – historians trying to quarrel with metaphysicians on phenomenological grounds and theological metaphysicians criticizing historians for metaphysical reasons. It is never possible to interpret phenomena in terms of phenomena. Always there is required some ground and principle that refer beyond the mere appearance and factuality of phenomena to some kind of meaning that the phenomena express.

Thus the characteristic Christian hypothesis lies beyond the competence of the merely historical verdict. Certainly we must use historical evidence to verify it to a certain extent, but we cannot expect that it will go all the way. There are inevitably metaphysical and existential elements involved in Christian faith, in so far as we consider and analyze it as a rational act made by a rational being (and, as we have seen, no other being except a rational being is capable of making any act of faith at all). The Christian hypothesis both completes and supplies the ground and basic motif of a metaphysic. At the same time it provides a profound and consistent account of human existence, of its ultimate purpose and being, and of Him in relation to whom we exist. Thus the characteristic hypothesis of Christian faith is formulated in terms of metaphysics, verified in terms of history, and entered into and enjoyed, translating itself into the immediacies of living experience, in existential and pragmatic terms. The relationship of history to faith is thus extremely important but certainly not more important than metaphysical thought and existential experience. Theology is indeed a metaphysic of history, but it is also a metaphysic of existence, and in the last resort simply a metaphysic. It gains enormously, of course, from its intimate connection with history and existence, borrowing from them a resonance and a relevance that other metaphysical systems lack, but it does not on that account forfeit its status as a metaphysic.

To say all this is to put history and historical research in its proper place as far as the Christian doctrine and interpretation of Jesus are concerned. The proper place of history is a very important one, but it is not on that account the paramount one. Obviously the basic Christian hypothesis of the incarnation and the incarnate life intertwines with history at many points, some of which at least can be strongly validated and reinforced by historical research. It is agreed by almost every kind of competent investigator that there was a religious teacher and reformer named Jesus of Nazareth, and that he was indeed crucified under Pontius Pilate. There is certainly some historical evidence that he was born of a virgin and rose from the dead, but the scrupulous historian is quite justified in saying that this evidence is not sufficient for him to affirm these things merely as the conclusions of laborious historical research. The evidence exists, and it is certainly far from nothing, but on the other hand, it could reasonably be pronounced insufficient. But the total Christian hypothesis, so illuminating metaphysically and compelling existentially, requires not only the glorious life and magnificent death but also the virginal conception and birth and the physical resurrection from the dead.

We have to ask ourselves whether the evidence that validates the life and the death merely validates the life and the death or reinforces the entire hypothesis. If we conceive a historical hypothesis A–B–C–D, with the evidences for B and C very strong but those for A and D less compelling, we have then to consider whether the evidences for B and C merely support B and C or whether in fact they assist us in verifying the entire hypothesis A–B–C–D. In the case of very few hypotheses that take a complex form like A–B–C–D is the empirical evidence equally strong at every point. Usually we have to be content with verifying the hypothesis at the points at which verification can reasonably be expected and procured, and rely upon the profound integration of the whole hypothesis, the mutual coherence and interrelatedness of its parts, to carry those elements of the hypothesis for which, in the nature of the case, verification can hardly be expected and certainly not demanded. In historical research this situation presents itself again and again, and it is by no means peculiar to the dilemmas of the interpreter of the New Testament. Certainly we do find in the basic Christian hypothesis a high degree of coherence and mutual interrelatedness between the parts, so that the evidence for those aspects of it which the historian can clearly see is also evidence — at a single remove, so to speak — for those portions of it which are more dimly discerned in a kind of historical twilight.

The general drift of this chapter has thus been to insist upon the importance of the philosophical and even the existential elements of historical decision. The trouble has often been that so many historians in the past have dreamed of the possibility of a kind of pure history, into which questions of philosophy do not enter. Whether or not such a pure history is possible anywhere at any time is, to say the least, doubtful, but quite certainly a pure history of this kind must be hopelessly inadequate whenever we are concerned with a highly metaphysical, existential question like the proper interpretation of the data that confront us in the New Testament. Hence, it is not surprising to discover that in the long run the kind of New Testament interpretation characteristic of modernistic and liberal Christianity during the last hundred years depends in the last resort upon philosophical attitudes rather than upon the results and conclusions of historical research. Our next task is inevitably therefore some discussion of the philosophical affiliations of the liberal theologians.

Chapter V

The Critique of Liberalism:
(2) Its Misuse of Philosophy

The principal contention of this chapter, though it must receive from us considerable elaboration and detailed exposition, may nevertheless be summarized very briefly at the outset. From the standpoint of philosophy the chief weakness of all forms of liberal theology known to me, and perhaps of all its possible forms, is a chronic tendency to try to combine a naturalistic interpretation of nature, which conceives of it as a self-contained whole and excludes the possibility of the supernatural or the miraculous, with a religious or existentialist interpretation of the life of man, which sees in it an area of being and activity in which some kind of divine initiative, or at least some kind of genuine relationship to God, is a live possibility. The interpretation of nature is conceded to the natural sciences while the interpretation of man is claimed for a liberal theology allied to an existentialist or spiritual philosophy. It will be our purpose clearly to demonstrate (a) that such a combination of naturalism and existentialism is impossible and (b) that so desperate a holding action in apologetics is quite unnecessary. It is not merely that naturalism is the correct and overwhelmingly cogent philosophical interpretation of nature and natural science, which somehow perversely breaks down when we turn to the interpretation of human existence, so that for this latter purpose we require a different philosophy altogether. The point is that naturalism fails even as an interpretation of nature and physics.

Basically this attempt to combine a naturalistic interpretation of nature with some sort of spiritual or existentialist account of man is dualistic. Reality and the whole structure of human experience is cut ruthlessly into two parts, each of which requires a different philosophy to interpret it. Historically we must interpret this intellectual phenomenon as a survival of the ancient dualistic Manichaean heresy in a new form.

The public history of the Manichaean heresies that menaced Christendom during the Dark and Middle Ages closes with the sad story of the destruction and extirpation of the Catharistic movement. There is considerable evidence, however, that tendencies of this kind survived, particularly during the later Middle Ages, among the commercial bourgeois of the new and growing medieval cities who were the ancestors of our modern middle classes. It was upon this bourgeois class that the Reformation doctrines and movements of the sixteenth century established their most considerable hold. In later Protestant history Manichaean influences can be traced in the strength of middle-class puritan movements and more recently in the vogue of liberal theology. In Roman Catholicism similar post-Manichaean dualistic tendencies can be traced, from Pascal onward, in Jansenism and in those Jansenistic tendencies which have survived the collapse of the heresy itself. Vague vestiges of Manichaeism are still very much alive in contemporary Western culture, as, for example, in the predominantly middle-class vogue of a cult like Christian Science and in the many brands of idealistic philosophy, like the transcendentalist movement, which somehow contrive to reassure their devotees that ultimately all reality is spirit.

The general tendency in the earlier history of Manichaean movements is for them to move secretly and furtively in the dim recesses of our culture, only manifesting themselves in the light of historical day every now and then in some big attempt to dominate a society such as we find in the Bogomils and the Catharists. Elsewhere Manichaeism can only be detected by conjecture. What I am suggesting here is that the affiliation of the basic heresies characteristic of liberal theology is with Manichaean dualism. In other words, the liberal theology is the characteristic form taken by the Manichaean heresy in the twentieth century. It has always been the way of Manichaeism to infiltrate Christianity subtly from within rather than to attack it from without, except in the rare circumstance in which it became very strong and confident, as, for example, in France during the twelfth and thirteenth centuries.

Of course, another influence derives from eighteenth-century deism. Although nature naturalistically interpreted is a closed system and a highly integrated continuum free from new divine initiative, yet it may still be represented as itself a divine initiative. God created the universe so perfectly, and so entirely is he satisfied with his work, that further initiatives are not so much impossible as infinitely unlikely because, so we are told, if God undertook such further initiatives it would imply that his first creative work is defective. In other words, God took an initiative in the beginning of such perfection that no further divine initiative is required. The result is a picture of life from which God is remote and absent, except in so far as we allow the possibility of divine initiative in intellectual and spiritual experience, in revelation, in morals, in justification and sanctification.

Rigid deism, of course, finds it difficult to make even these latter exceptions. Deism is a doctrine that derives from the eighteenth century, the great age of Newtonian physics, though it has its roots in the seventeenth century and particularly in Galileo. From this point of view the new physics establishes that the universe is a closed system and an integrated continuum, permitting only of such interpretations and schematisms as we find in mathematical physics. There are only two things that mathematical physics cannot explain and is not capable of explaining: how this universe got going in the first place and how it gets itself known in the second place. This gives us two realities that it is beyond the power of the new

physics to interpret: God who gets the universe going and
the human consciousness that knows it. Apart from these two
realities, all is physics, and what is described in physics is a
closed mathematical system that remains eternally the same,
which has neither history nor evolution.

It was Darwin who destroyed this picture and compelled
us to think in terms of an evolving universe in which novelty
repeatedly occurs. It is a strange paradox that nineteenth-
century theologians in general did not welcome the advent of
Darwin. If they had been more concerned with the adequacy
of traditional Christian theology and less concerned about the
precise historicity of Genesis, their attitude would not only
have been very different but also much more intelligent. If
eighteenth-century physics led to the idea of the closed universe, nineteenth-century Darwinian biology pointed toward
the idea of the open universe, open at all events toward the
future. We can trace this dualism in Hegel and in almost all
nineteenth-century thought. Nature is a necessity that has no
history; and history, conceived in the dynamic, evolutionist
way, is a freedom that has no nature. Even contemporary
existentialism is very largely taken up with refuting notions of
any kind of fixed or universal human nature.

Yet there is nothing particularly contemporary in all this,
for as long ago as Plato's *Timaeus* we were told that the creation is mixed, being compounded of necessity and freedom.
Such a dualism inevitably requires two separate philosophies
in order to do justice to its needs: a necessitarian naturalism
to interpret nature, and some kind of free existentialism or
spiritualism to interpret man and mind. Thus in modern
thought and terminology we find our way back to something
very like the double truth theory, the vogue of which we have
already observed in the thirteenth century.

Yet there are very good reasons for supposing that any philosophical dualism of this kind is inherently unsatisfactory. We
are confronted by a naturalistic account of nature on the one
hand and an existentialist account of man and mind on the

other. Such a formulation might be possible if man and mind were merely in nature and if nature were in no sense to be found in man and mind. But the fact is that nature is not merely the context of human life and history, it is also ingredient into human life and history. To be a man is not merely to be in the world, it is also to recognize the existence of the world in oneself. Man recapitulates in himself the whole evolution of creation; there is a physics of man and a biology of man, and when man knows himself, what he knows is not merely his spiritual existence but also his physics and biology. In knowing himself he inevitably knows nature in himself, experiencing its sharp physical pulls and necessities. To be man is to be what the naturalist calls nature, just as much as it is to be what the existentialist calls existence. Man is the being in whom the dualism of nature and existence is overcome, and therefore he is certainly not the being who can logically and intelligently commit the dualistic fallacy. To be man is to be the being who knows within himself that dualism cannot be true.

One way by which the dualists seek to evade this difficulty is to provide a dualistic account of man himself, a picture of man as a combination of mind, or soul, and body joined together in a manner that is either unintelligible, or inconceivable, or at least ineluctably paradoxical — as for merely philosophical dualists — or downright scandalous — as for religious or Manichaean dualists. In either case the bifurcation of reality in the last resort results in a bifurcation of man, for man is the point at which the naturalistic and the existential meet and find themselves embarrassingly one.

Now the point of this brief analysis is not merely that the dualism of the naturalistic and the existential is impossible. If that were so, we might conceivably evade the difficulty either by opting for total naturalism, including a naturalistic account of man, or a total existentialism, including some kind of existential account of nature. And indeed it is probably true that we can find analogies to existentialism in nature and analogies to naturalism in existence. Nevertheless the naturalist is probably correct when he tells us that there cannot be an existentialist interpretation of nature and natural science, and the existentialist equally correct when he refutes and rejects all naturalistic interpretations of man. My point would be rather different; what this analysis betrays is the fact that neither naturalism nor existentialism is philosophically acceptable. Naturalism fails because it is so obviously a hopelessly inadequate interpretation of existence; existentialism is inadequate for precisely the opposite reason, because it cannot even begin to function as a philosophy of nature. Dualism fails because it cannot do justice to the fact that ours is after all one world, in which indeed things exist in a profusion of variety, but in which also all the many varieties interpenetrate on the levels of both experience and of being. The slogan of the philosopher must necessarily be "one philosophy for one world." Such a basic rule of philosophical thought makes any sort of dualism impossible.

Dualism commits a further error. Nature and existence are not the only grades, levels, or dimensions of our experience. Even within our own self-conscious being, there intervenes between nature and personal existence the world of history-society-culture, and we may well inquire of the naturalist whether this historical world is to be interpreted existentially and of the existentialist, who is usually very suspicious of the way in which social and cultural norms threaten the independence of individual personality, whether it had not better be interpreted naturalistically. It would seem to me obvious that history-society-culture cannot with success be interpreted either naturalistically or existentially. In other words, as a mode of reality it is distinct from both nature on the one hand and personal existence on the other. History is certainly in nature, and it certainly accommodates and fosters existence, yet, nevertheless, it cannot plausibly be reduced to either.

Certainly in Christian thought, as in Biblical testimony, the Christ who is the living revelation of God exists on all three levels of human experience at once. He is present within nature as miracle — and this is for us the primary significance of the virgin birth and the empty tomb, the passage of the Son of God through the whole life of the creation begins and ends in miracle precisely because it is a miracle; he is present on the level of history-society-culture as revelation; and he is present on the level of existence as grace; for the graciousness of God is, above all, made manifest in the gift of the incarnate Lord. If this formulation is correct, then there can be no possible evasion of the problem of miracle. No one problem has so preoccupied the Christian apologists during the last two hundred years, and it is to this perennial perplexity that we now turn.

Some people would seek to define miracle as an interruption of an otherwise invariable cause and effect sequence so that miracle might also be defined as a kind of uncaused event. But this is quite clearly an incorrect procedure. The miraculous event must most definitely have a cause, and if miracles do in fact occur, the cause and effect sequence is clearly not so rigid and invariable as it was once customary to suppose. If miracles occur at any particular point in space time, they are no more unintelligible per se than nonmiraculous events at other points in space time. Miraculous events may differ from nonmiraculous events in that they require the application of different categories and hypotheses in order to render them intelligible, but they do not differ from them by being unintelligible per se. Thus the categories that render the process of physical decomposition in the tomb intelligible are clearly distinct from the categories that render the resurrection of Christ intelligible, just as the categories that help us to understand the resurrection of Christ do not assist us to understand and interpret the normal physical decomposition of dead bodies. But given the use of the appropriate categories of interpretation, each of these events is equally intelligible, and one is seen to be in no way incompatible with the other.

Miracle might perhaps be defined as an event of whose cause we are unaware. From this point of view, an airplane would be a miraculous event for the unsophisticated mind of the primitive man. Indeed, if a miracle is simply an observed event of which we do not know the cause, then the airplane is miraculous for most civilized men, for very few of us in this age of aeronautics are equipped with the technical knowledge that would enable us understand precisely what it is that keeps the plane poised steadily in the air thousands of feet above the ground. No doubt this is what people have in mind when they talk, as they sometimes do, of "the miracles of modern science." This is indeed a scientific and technical age in a very important sense and to an unparalleled degree, but nevertheless the great majority of those who live in the scientific age are neither scientists nor technicians, so that in this sense of the word "miracle" we do indeed find ourselves surrounded by miracles.

There is an important analogy between technology and miracle on which perhaps we should dwell more than we do, if only because it may assist people to accept the category of miracle with their understanding in the environment of a technical age. Modern technology, after all, although distinct from science, is nevertheless based upon it. The stupendous achievements of modern technics remind us of the fact that knowledge of and about the ways of the natural creation brings with it a certain power to shape and mold it to some extent nearer to our heart's desire. Knowledge, even our finite knowledge with its many gaps and intellectual imperfections, confers power upon the knower. If this is true of the finite creature's knowledge of the creation in which he finds himself and by which his life is in the last resort conditioned, how much more, we may well ask ourselves, must it be true of the Creator's absolute knowledge of a creation that he transcends? If men know enough about the nature of things at least plausibly to imagine themselves the "masters of things," in their more aspiring, rhetorical moods, can they deny God that absolute mastery of things which makes the miracle possible? Men are indeed somewhat the masters of things, as this technical age reminds us again and again. Are we not therefore compelled to ascribe to God by analogy an absolute mastery of things?

It is surely illogical and absurd to suppose that man as scientist and technician can to some extent mold nature to his purposes, and yet at the same time conceive of the order of nature as something that absolutely limits the will and purpose of its Creator. Usually those who have dwelt upon what they suppose to be scientific reasons for rejecting the concept and category of miracle have in mind primarily the concept of science as a rigid system of thought. If, however, we think of science in terms of the technical activity and mastery that it makes possible, the analogy may well tell in the opposite direction.

We might refine this definition of miracle by saying that it is an event the cause of which we not only *do* not know but *can*not know. This definition will be found equally unsatisfactory. Theology does not claim to know all about the causation of the miraculous events that enter into its subject matter, but it does claim that it is possible to know enough about their causation to render them intelligible. Even if we knew all about the causation of the miraculous event, it would still be a miraculous event. It takes more than the mere fact of our ignorance of the causal process that produces the miracle to make the miracle a miracle.

Perhaps it might be better to say that a miracle is a uniquely caused event, i.e., an event brought about through the causal agency of a unique being with unique purposes. Certainly if an utterly unique being were to be present in the world we should expect some strikingly unique consequences of such a presence to make themselves manifest before our eyes. The idea that a unique causal agency should operate without any unique effects whatever is certainly a quite unintelligible and even self-contradictory one.

Another and more traditional way of approaching the definition of miracle is to call it a " supernatural " event. The term " supernatural " is not very popular among contemporary theo-

logians, and it must be confessed that they have some reason
for regarding it with suspicion. It is so closely associated with
that antitheological, antirational trend in some types of Christian thought which seems to regard the supernatural as
synonymous with the unintelligible. Certainly theology must
reject any crude identification of the supernatural with the unintelligible. On the other hand, it cannot conceivably, in my
view, reject the conception of the supernatural altogether.
Rather, it is the function of theology to show that the supernatural has made itself intelligible, and is seen to have made
itself intelligible, by so manifesting itself as to permit or render possible the processes and categories of theological thinking. God is certainly not a part of nature. Indeed, it is not even
permissible, without careful qualification, to ascribe to God
the possession of a nature, for a nature is always something
that several distinct existences share in common. Thus the existence of God is itself a supernatural reality. In the same way,
if there are any events or processes in which God takes the
initiative and intervenes in the area of human existence and
experience, then all such events and processes must be described as supernatural, whether they are miraculous or not.
This is perhaps the real objection to defining the miracle
merely as a supernatural event. If all events in which God takes
a direct initiative are supernatural, then clearly the great majority of such events are not miraculous in any ordinary and
generally accepted sense of the word.

It should be noted that the term " supernatural " in no sense
connotes anything unnatural or contrary to nature. If supernatural events occur, then they occur within a natural context,
and the realm of the natural provides such events with their essential raw material. The realm of the natural could not of itself produce such events, but it is not of such a character as to
forbid or to render impossible their production. Similarly the
realm of the natural could not of itself produce a Beethoven
symphony. Nevertheless, it is clear that the realm of the natural is not so constituted as to render the production of a

Beethoven symphony impossible. (Incidentally, the question really arises whether or not we should regard the Beethoven symphony as a supernatural event, or, at least as an *extra*-natural or *a*natural event. For the Beethoven symphony, like all works of the creative genius in man, is not the product of the human nature that Beethoven shares with us all, but rather the product of that which was peculiar to Beethoven, his own Beethovenish identity and personality. It is the work of his singularity rather than of his generality. In this sense all those human creative activities which must be defined in terms of the singularity of the Creator, rather than in terms of the general potentialities of the human race, may properly be called *super-* or *extra-* or *a*-natural, for they are not the consequence of our nature but the consequence of our singularity.) The main conclusion here, however, is that although a miracle is certainly a supernatural event, it cannot be defined merely as a supernatural event, because so many supernatural events are not events we should normally describe as miraculous.

Another approach to the definition of miracle may be through the important distinction between contextual and dramatic explanation. Contextual explanation interprets events and behavior in terms of the characteristic laws of the field or area in which the events or behavior occurs. " This," we say, " is the kind of thing that repeatedly occurs within this kind of context." (E.g., we are not surprised that most of the people who visit a dancing studio go there with the purpose of dancing or learning to dance.) Dramatic explanation, however, explains an event or action in terms of the singular purposes and intentions of the agent. Thus we explain the fact that debates continually occur in the British House of Commons contextually, but we explain the fact that in some particular debate the Prime Minister made quite an unexpected speech in terms of his policies, ultimate intentions, character, and distressing situation. In the light of this distinction we might attempt a threefold classification of all events:

A. Events that are susceptible of a contextual explanation only.

B. Events that are capable of both contextual and dramatic explanation at the same time. (E.g., the Beethoven symphony may be explained in part as a result of the operation of the unique genius of Beethoven, but it must also be explained in part contextually in terms of the previous history of music, the technical development of the symphony orchestra, and the general character of German, and particularly Viennese, culture around about the beginning of the nineteenth century.)

C. Events that are incapable of any other but a dramatic explanation, so that the context of such events simply functions as a mere context, without contributing anything to the explanation whatsoever.

The first of these three classes of events may be called purely natural events in the primary sense. The second consists of supernatural events that nevertheless have a natural character, of supernatural events that are nonmiraculous. The third consists of supernatural events that are also miraculous, of events that, so to speak, have *no nature,* but are explicable and intelligible purely in terms of their singularity.

We have thus reached the point at which it is possible to define miracle. The miraculous is pure singularity; it is the event that has no nature, that belongs to no well-marked and definable class of events; an event that is seen to be intelligible only in terms of itself. Again it should be noted that the miracle is in no sense unnatural or contrary to nature. It is simply that neither our existing knowledge of the natural, nor any future knowledge of the natural which we may hope to attain, can shed the slightest light on its character or in any way explain its occurrence. In a sense this means that the miracle has no definition; rather, by subsuming it under the category of the singular we define it negatively in terms of its nonsusceptibility to any kind of definition. The realm of the definitive is clearly the realm of the natural, since it is in terms of their natures that things are classified, and the classes to which they belong defined.

Our observations so far have another very important implication. The miraculous is not unnatural or contrary to nature precisely because nature is *not a closed system*. The realm of nature is not closed to miracle because it is not closed to the creative activity of the God who created it. To suppose that once we have exhaustively explored the realm of the natural and correctly defined all its constituent and operative natures we shall see it as a completely closed system is to conceive and define the creation as though it were, so to speak, God's strait jacket. Even if we leave the data provided by religious revelation completely out of account, and consider reality simply as known to natural science and in human existence, it is clear that nature is not closed to the unique. Again, the biological concept of evolution compels any kind of philosophical naturalism to conceive and embrace the concept of the openness of nature, its openness to novelty and to new, unforeseen, and unforeseeable developments. Similarly any analysis of human existence forces upon our attention the actuality of unique elements within the present context of the natural itself. It is on the basis of this insistence, that the realm of the natural is not a closed system, that we can embark upon the next phase of this discussion.

Having defined miracle in terms of its singularity and its demand for purely dramatic, nonconceptual explanation, we are now in a position to consider the intellectual prejudice against the category of miracle so widespread in the contemporary climate of opinion. At one time it was customary for many thinkers to set miracle dogmatically aside as impossible, as contrary to some concept of an invariable reign of a law of known cause and effect throughout the entire length and breadth of the empirical world. Nowadays we are perhaps less inclined to be quite so dogmatic about invariable chains of cause and effect, and we usually prefer to speak in terms of

statistical probability and improbability — a most striking intellectual advance. From this later point of view miracle is not
so much impossible as almost infinitely improbable.

The concept of the impossible is a radically unscientific one,
for it denies by implication the priority of fact over theory. We
can only declare an alleged fact, however well attested, impossible in the name of some theory based on our experience
of other well-attested facts. If a miracle occurs, then clearly
miracles are not impossible. Even if no sufficiently well-attested
miracle has as yet ever occurred, miracle remains possible. The
proper concern of science is to weigh the facts of experience
and to interpret them in appropriate categories which manifest
their appropriateness by displaying their capacity to interpret
them. Science has nothing to do with the censorship or sup-
pression of inconvenient facts. If a fact cannot be explained or
interpreted by one set of categories, then we must turn to some
other set of categories in terms of which it will reveal its in-
telligibility.

The notion of the impossible is really based on a combination
of two indefensible presuppositions: (1) the dogma that nature
is a closed system, which is incompatible with immediate existential experience, and with a general interpretation of our
best and most universally received scientific doctrines; and
(2) the presumption that we already know enough about the
character of this closed system to dogmatize about the possi-
bilities that it excludes — and this is to sin against the noblest
virtue of the scientific mind, its profound humility in the face
of empirical reality.

To explore more deeply still, we may say that behind the
concept of the impossibility of miracle there lies a confusion
between the logical character of empirical science and the
methodological convictions of rationalist philosophy. The impossible is a confused apprehension on the level of empirical
science of the concept of the self-contradictory in rationalist
philosophy. Thus the philosopher might say, rightly enough,
that a square circle is impossible because it is self-contradic-

tory. But the category of the miraculous is very different from the category of the self-contradictory. There is nothing in common between the resurrection and the square circle. If the square circle is square, then it is not a circle; and if it is circular, it cannot be a square. The self-contradictory is a category of purely rationalistic philosophy to which there is nothing analogous in the realm of empirical science. Nevertheless, in the nineteenth century the category of the impossible was used by philosophical interpreters of the spirit and the results of empirical science in the same, or at least an analogous, way as the category of the self-contradictory employed by the rationalist philosopher. This is a confusion from which we have been delivered by a better appreciation of the character of empirical knowledge in the twentieth century. Philosophical interpreters of empirical science no longer feel it necessary to employ basic dogmas like the uniformity of nature or the invariable laws of cause and effect. Instead they substitute the humbler, more agnostic, notion of degrees of probability and improbability.

This leads us to our second and intellectually more respectable question: Are miracles infinitely improbable? To this it must be replied that even for those who point to certain miracles as supremely significant they must certainly be regarded as very improbable indeed and extremely rare. Episodes like the resurrection and the virgin birth would have almost no significance at all, or at least a very different significance, if human beings were rising from the dead and being born of virgins every day of the week. The extreme rarity of the miracle is an essential ingredient in its significance. On the other hand, the category of the infinitely improbable is rhetorical and intellectually imprecise. It can mean no more than extremely or very improbable. From the standpoint of any generalized mathematical theory of the degrees of probability and improbability it is probable that, if a sufficiently large number of relevant events occur, some of these events will be improbable, even extremely improbable, ones.

The fact is that the improbable does occur. Bishop Butler was trembling on the verge of this observation when he asked the question: What is the probability that any particular infant, "mewling and puking in its cradle," will grow up into Julius Caesar and live out the precise career of Julius Caesar as known to history? The answer is clearly that it must always have been very improbable that any particular infant would grow up into Julius Caesar. Indeed all the particular and singular events of history must be reckoned as extremely improbable, for at every point in human history there are so many possible alternatives that the selection of any one of them is bound to be somewhat surprising. In fact, of course, one particular infant did grow up to be Julius Caesar. But we do not need to select an outstanding career like that of Julius Caesar in order to demonstrate the point. Any mature man can ask himself, "What was the probability that any particular infant born round about the time of my birth would grow up into the man I have become, achieve what I have achieved, and make the mistakes that I have made?" The answer is that whatever the achievements and whatever the mistakes it was extremely improbable. If we survey a ward full of infants in a maternity hospital, the probability of any of them growing up to live precisely the life that any one of them will subsequently live must be rated extremely low. The theory of probability and improbability thus gives us no warrant for supposing that the improbable will not occur. The most that we can say from the standpoint of this theory is that the improbable will only occur very rarely, perhaps even that some probabilities — e.g., the improbabilities that compose an actual human existence — will only occur uniquely.

It is perhaps important to note parenthetically that the concept of degrees of probability and improbability is a much wider and all-embracing one than the mathematical concept of a calculable probability. It is only possible to calculate probability or improbability mathematically within very fixed limits, and in relation to peculiarly appropriate subject matters. It is possible, for example, to calculate the probability that in randomly selecting a single card from a deck of cards I shall turn up the ace of spades, only because it is previously known that the deck contains only fifty-two cards. The probability or improbability of the singular events and episodes of history — e.g., that a particular infant will grow up to be Julius Caesar — cannot be calculated in this way. Thus we must distinguish between the calculable probability and probability considered as a philosophical concept. In this discussion we have been using it only in the latter sense.

Of course, it is always possible that the typically "modern" man will react to this kind of analysis emotionally, almost existentially, rather than rationally. "Whatever the Christian philosopher may say," he will reply, "and however well he may say it, a miracle is something in which I simply cannot believe. Even though I could think of no very good reason for my inability to believe in it, the fact remains that I am psychologically incapable of doing so. To me a miracle is simply incredible." Here we are getting to the very heart of the modern difficulty about miracle. It is not a difficulty experienced by a purely rational man when he is, so to speak, "alone with his reason" and his thought is determined by reasoning alone. It is, on the contrary, a difficulty peculiar to man subject to the pressure and presuppositions of a particular culture and climate of opinion. It is social rather than rational in its origin. This social and cultural rejection of miracle will often attempt to mask itself behind an elaborate show of rationalization, but even when rational analysis has exposed the rationalization, and made manifest what it really is, the intellectual block may well survive in a starkly unrationalized form. It may then assert itself as a kind of intuition, instinct, or hunch, to which the modern intellectual may cling desperately even though, perhaps because, he has no other visible means of support.

People who try to defend Christian faith and belief as a kind of saving intuition, and sometimes interpret a defense of irrational intuition as though it were *ipso facto* a defense of Christian faith itself, would do well to remember that there may be intuitionist arguments of this kind for the rejection of Christianity. The trouble with irrationalism is that it is an easy game that every man knows how to play. We hear too much in modern religious discussion of alleged motivations and considerations that are defined as "above reason" or suprarational. In human existence there is no type of mental process that is above or superior to reason. Mental processes are either rational or in some significant way below the level of reason. The suprarational does not and cannot exist; only the subrational. It is the animals who are irrational, not the angels.

What has a man really in mind when he finds it difficult or impossible to believe in some particular idea or assertion even though he may have no very clear rational objection to it? He may of course mean that he finds it difficult or impossible to believe in X because it is for him inconceivable that it could be true. But if it really is inconceivable, he should be rationally capable of stating precisely why it is that he finds it inconceivable. The story of the resurrection is clearly not inconceivable in the sense that the proposition "two plus two equals five" is inconceivable. The inconceivable is that which involves rational self-contraction, and this cannot be said a priori of any particular miracle story. He may mean, however, and in my view this is always in the last analysis what he does mean, that he finds it difficult and impossible to believe in X because it is for him unimaginable, so unlike the general run of his own immediate experience that he cannot imagine its being true.

The Christian will do well to take a sympathetic view of a profound psychological difficulty of this kind. He has the great advantage of seeing the great Gospel miracle from the point of view of Christian existence with and under Christ in the church. It is not in the least difficult for him to imagine the truth of the Gospel miracles, precisely because they do not cut across the general tenor of his immediate experience. From the point of view of a man who has been receiving and adoring the risen Christ in the Eucharist for many years there is no particular psychological difficulty in *imagining* the resurrection. On the contrary, it coheres so profoundly with his immediate experience of life that he affirms the fact almost lightheartedly and without any sense of having to overcome any kind of mental block. Yet for another man, whose circumstances and situation are very different, the block may be a very formidable one indeed, and we should take a very sympathetic attitude toward his difficulty.

What we must do here, however, is to distinguish radically between the unimaginable and inconceivable. Not only in theology but also in philosophy and natural science it is often necessary to conceive the unimaginable. Thus it is very difficult — for most, perhaps for all, well-nigh impossible — to *imagine* the physical universe as it is schematically reconstructed for us by modern relativity physics, yet at the same time it is scientifically possible and necessary to *conceive* it. Again and again in reading books about modern physics and astronomy the imagination is amazed at the wonders and the infinitudes that are revealed. Yet always the success of the scientific quest demands that the rational intellect should persevere steadily through this " dark night of the imagination " in the service of and the search for truth. Again and again we find that the unimaginable is nevertheless conceivable, and that it is reason itself which bids us embrace and hold fast to these austere intellectual beauties.

Perhaps we may conclude this discussion of the problem of miracle by insisting upon its apologetic relevance and importance. Particularly for those influenced by naturalistic modes of thought, the demonstration of God's lordship over and domination of nature, which any miracle reveals and declares, is of tremendous significance if they are to move away from a philosophy that thinks in terms of merely impersonal natural necessity and pass over into an affirmation of the ultimate sovereignty in life of personal purpose and meaning. The problem of miracle has for so long been an embarrassment to apologists that it may seem a little strange and paradoxical to assert that miracle has an actual place, and that an important one, in the actual work of apologetic communication to the modern mind. Miracle is not merely something of an intellectual scandal to be explained away. On the contrary, the fact that miracles have occurred, and even do sometimes occur, is now seen to be essential to Christian communication and to the Christian affirmation of the sovereign freedom of God. Thus, for example, Donald M. Mackinnon, in analyzing the essential content of what must be urged by Christians in their dialogue with communism, strongly stresses the immense relevance of the great Biblical and Christian affirmation of the empty tomb:

> The empty tomb, for instance, is not a kind of optional appendage to the Christian message: It lies at its very heart. The material aspirations of Marxism can only be met by a faith that proclaims a deed done in flesh and blood and issuing in a real transformation of that in which it was done.[10]

The Communists, in other words, make their appeal to the reality of matter, and it is to the reality of matter they must go. The Christians also affirm the reality of the material universe: they proclaim its reality solemnly in the Nicene Creed, and they use material realities boldly for spiritual purposes in their sacraments. But whereas for the Communists matter is an absolute reality, for the Christian it is a contingent reality, with a contingency made dramatically manifest in miracle. True, it is possible to show that the material universe is and must be a contingent reality by metaphysical analysis, but metaphysical analysis lacks the striking manifestation and conclusive evidence that miracle supplies. Part of the conversion of the materialist lies in this revelation to him that even his favorite material world is constrained at times to acknowledge the mastery and proclaim the glory of God.

As we have already seen, it must always be impossible to combine a naturalist, contextual account of nature with the dramatic, existentialist account of man. If the old world of naturalism is unbalanced, we cannot hope to redress the balance by calling upon this new world of existentialism. Bultmann needs both naturalism and existentialism. The naturalism tells him that the supernatural stories contained in the Gospels are mythical, while the existentialism, as if by a kind of conjuring trick, enables him to supply them with some kind of kerygmatic-existentialist interpretation of their meaning. But whereas the metaphysical implications of naturalism point toward an ultimate reality that is impersonal, his existentialism, by the same kind of necessity, points toward the priority and ultimate supremacy of personality. The kind of existence which existentialism describes is hardly compatible with the sort of essence which naturalism defines. From the standpoint of naturalism what we know as existence emerges out of nature and can hardly be conceived as so foreign to its native soil as it must be if it is as the existentialist depicts it. From the standpoint of existentialism nature is, after all, the context of existence, of our being in the world; is indeed, in the last resort, a concept that arises in the minds of existing individuals in the course of their reflection upon their existentially conditioned career. It can hardly be so alien to the complex make-up of the existing individual who thinks it as the naturalist would suppose.

In the long run we cannot be satisfied with less than one philosophy, one center and source of interpretation for one world. It is in terms of this philosophy that both nature and existence must be interpreted. Thus a philosophy of nature that cannot interpret existence is not even a good philosophy of nature, for existence occurs within the context of nature and indeed emerges out of it. Even so, a philosophy of existence that cannot interpret the actuality of nature is not even a good philosophy of existence, for natural science only emerges in the context of the thought of existential man straining, with a deeply subjective passion and craving for objective knowledge, toward which the human thinker gravitates as surely as the phototropic creature moves toward the light. For there is indeed such a subjective craving for the objective, and the existentialist ignores and neglects it at his peril.

Of course it is true that the great majority of Christian lay people and ministers ignore and set aside the kind of liberal theological constructions we have been discussing. Sometimes they have never heard of them, but even those who have heard of them usually pass them by, rather as the working modern scientist tosses into his wastepaper basket the new book pleading for the flat earth theory after little more than a cursory examination. It is so far outside his life, experience, and presuppositions that he instantly rejects it, almost without examination.

Sometimes, however, faithful persons of this kind are really worried by the liberal theology. They see clearly enough, and no doubt they are usually right, that the liberal theologians are much more intelligent and widely informed than they are. They tell themselves either that the Bible is God's book, and that God is much more likely to be right than the liberal theologian, or that the church has a long and glorious theological tradition which has been inspired by the Holy Spirit, and that the church is much more likely to be right than the liberal theologians. I understand and sympathize with reactions of this kind, but they seem to me inadequate. It is the contention of this book that the liberal form of theology has sinned not only against God, the Bible, and historic faith but also against reason. The liberal theology does not reflect long and seriously enough either about the nature of history or about the philosophical foundations of the characteristically liberal theology. It is very clear that liberalism in theology is religiously inadequate, but let us spare a moment in which to observe that it is philosophically disastrous also. If liberalism fails appallingly to communicate Christianity to the world, this is perhaps in part because too little of Christianity remains in liberalism to make it worth communicating, and in part also because, in the ivory towers that the liberals inhabit, so little is known or understood of the actual world and its intellectual needs.

Chapter VI

The Effectiveness of
Contemporary Apologetics

Of course, there are those who deny the validity of any apologetic ministry whatsoever. " It is impossible," we are told, " to argue any man into becoming a Christian." The act of faith is not a mere deducing of the correct conclusion from the relevant premises even when we are agreed as to what they are. The act of faith is a response to the gospel, a response neither merely of the intellect nor merely of the will but of the whole man, including both intellect and will. Like the gospel to which it responds, the act of faith is a supernatural event, for, if the hand of God is explicit in the stimulus, the hand of God is at least implicit also in the response. The act of faith, indeed, is not the solution of the intellectual problems with which Christianity confronts us, rather, it is the cause of them. The intellectual problems of a man without faith are fewer and less profound than those of the man possessed by faith, so that faith is an enormous intellectual stimulus, at all events, when the faith in question is the faith of a temperamentally and vocationally intellectual type of man.

It must be confessed that the term " supernatural " has become, after centuries of loose usage, a somewhat ambiguous one. " Supernatural," as we have seen, does not mean nonnatural or antinatural. On the contrary, the supernatural always includes or recapitulates the natural. Thus the birth, life, and death and resurrection of Christ is a supernatural event, but it is also a natural event. Certainly it is no mere theophany, like

139

the sudden appearances of gods among men in many pagan mythologies. The supernatural is that which cannot be interpreted or accounted for merely in terms of its natural history, but this does not mean that it has no natural history. From the standpoint of Christian philosophy even the creation and existence of nature is a supernatural event, for there is nothing in our knowledge of God that makes the creation of nature necessary, although there is much in our knowledge of God that indicates that it is an eternal possibility.

Thus the supernatural is not so much nonnatural or antinatural as the more than natural, that overplus of reality in almost everything with which we are acquainted which brings it about that the description of anything that has any reality at all always transcends its definition, so that everything is more than it need be in order merely to be.

> O, reason not the need! our basest beggars
> Are in the poorest thing superfluous.
> Allow not nature more than nature needs,
> Man's life is cheap as beast's.[11]

On a lower level one is reminded of the reply of the French estate agent during the ancient regime, when a peasant excused himself for nonpayment of his rent by saying, " A man must live "; to whom the agent replied, " I don't perceive the necessity." Ethically we shall not care very much for this rejoinder, but theologically and metaphysically it is impeccable. The realm of the creation is the realm of the nonnecessary, in which the actuality of everything transcends its immanent idea. Thus even the natural itself is only a mode or expression of the supernatural, and certainly we can never say that because something or other is natural or has a natural characteristic it is therefore nonsupernatural. Hence although the act of faith always transcends the mere logic of the argument that leads up to it, that never means that the logic is unimportant or insignificant. Thus the supernatural character of faith does not exclude the validity and religious importance of rational apologetics. Man needs more than his mere nature to become a Christian, but he cannot become a Christian without or apart from his nature.

However, we must notice that there are two very distinct types of reason that may cause a man to refuse to commit himself in and to the act of faith. A man may refuse and reject Christian faith merely because he has examined Christianity itself and become convinced of some lack of evidence for it or of some kind of internal incoherence within it which permits him to reject it without necessarily affirming anything else. This state of mind is not unknown, but probably rather rare. The commoner condition is that of the man who refuses to make the act of Christian faith because he has already sincerely affirmed some other intellectual position that either is or seems to him to be incompatible with Christianity. This second attitude is both the commoner and the more defensible. There is, of course, a third possibility, of which we can have less to say in this chapter, although it is without doubt exceedingly important. There are those who suffer from what might almost be called a disease of the mind and the will which prevents them from entering upon any act of faith whatsoever, a kind of chronic skepticism, deadening the intellect and impoverishing the life, which atrophies the human potentiality for self-commitment. "Man," says Nietzsche "is the being who makes promises." Unfortunately he is also the dishonorable being who breaks them, and sometimes, even worse, the timid being who dares not make any. This kind of temperamental incapacity for any kind of faith at all is not, however, a primary elite characteristic. Among the elites, our second group — those who cannot affirm Christianity because they have affirmed something else incompatible with it — is incomparably the most common.

Now of course, in supposing that he cannot affirm Christianity because he has affirmed some alternative religious or metaphysical position incompatible with it, such a man may be mistaken, in which case the main work of apologetics may well be to isolate and diagnose his intellectual error and trace

it to its source. On the other hand, it is more likely to be the
case, where we are dealing with a man of real intellectual competence and integrity, that he is not mistaken, and that it is his
very real honesty which forbids him to affirm the Christian
faith so long as he continues to affirm something else incompatible with it. In this case the task of apologetics is to refute
the incompatible assumption. Such an apologetic does not attempt to demonstrate or establish the truth of Christianity,
rather, it strives to remove significant intellectual obstacles that
impede or even altogether close the pathway that leads to
Christianity. From this point of view it is for apologetics above
all to seize the intellectual initiative and to attack prevalent
and contemporary doctrines and ideas which, as long as men
believe in them, prevent them from becoming Christians.

Thus occasionally the apologist will say: "You are making a
bad mistake. The notion or doctrine which you suppose to be
incompatible with Christianity, and which you have felt compelled, either by the course of your own thought and experience, or because of the manifest authority of the evidences
adduced, to affirm, is not after all incompatible with Christian
belief, as we can easily discover by analyzing the content of
Christian affirmation with more insight and care than you appear to have used." More often, however, the apologist ought
to say: "You are making an enormous mistake. You are affirming something that close critical analysis will show to be an
error. The evidences do not support it, and if your own thinking has led you to this conclusion, it has been badly misin-
formed or misconceived, so that it is now your duty to deny
the position that you once affirmed."

Perhaps the greatest weakness of contemporary religious
apologists, however, is their tendency constantly to suppose
themselves in the former of these two intellectual situations
when they are in fact in the latter. The apologist understand-
ably experiences an urge to agree with those to whom he addresses himself so far as he possibly can, with the result that in
an excess of generosity and zeal he repeatedly goes too far and

affirms characteristically contemporary positions that ought not to be affirmed at all, not primarily because they are incompatible with Christianity, but primarily because a more profound philosophical analysis, a more careful scrutiny of the evidence, indicates that they ought not to be affirmed by anybody, whether Christian or not. The first failure of this kind of apologist is thus a failure of critical power, a failure to be sufficiently skeptical of fashionable intellectual vogues and contemporary beliefs. Every man is skeptical of something or other. No doubt the chronic skeptic is skeptical of everything, but this is still rather a rare and exotic disease. Most of us doubt what we doubt precisely because we are sure of what we are sure about, and this is the only kind of rational doubt there is. We must clearly distinguish between rational doubt and pathological doubt. The intelligent Christian is just as skeptical as the intelligent non-Christian. The only difference is that he is skeptical about different things. The Christian is assured where the non-Christian feels uncertain, and skeptical where the non-Christian feels sure of his ground.

Unfortunately for the apologist this persistent tendency to attempt to reconcile Christianity with incompatible positions, rather than critically to undermine and destroy the incompatibles, leads many of those who observe his performance, no doubt rather unfairly, to question his intellectual integrity. It appears to such people that the apologist, in his effort to persuade people that the positions they regard as incompatible with Christianity are not really incompatible with it after all, tends to produce his own version of Christianity, drastically blue-penciled, subedited, and reduced, and that this is not really the authentic Christianity of the central Christian tradition, or of the great majority of Christians at all. It is not surprising that many people feel that the Christian apologist is offering them counterfeit coin of his own manufacture, and they naturally feel somewhat irked when he persists in identifying this creature of his own brain with the objective, historic Christianity of the ages.

"The philosopher," said Kierkegaard in his *Concluding Un-scientific Postscript*, "contemplates Christianity for the sake of interpenetrating it with his speculative thought." [12] Later on in the same book we read again: "Speculative philosophy does not by any means say that Christianity is false; on the contrary, it says that speculative philosophy grasps the truth of Christianity. . . . It is not Christianity which is and was and remains the truth, and what the speculative philosopher understands is not that Christianity is the truth; no, it is the philosopher's understanding of Christianity that constitutes the truth of Christianity." [13]

The confusion to which Kierkegaard points is between an objective Christianity, however defined and whereinsoever contained, and a merely personal and subjective interpretation of Christianity. At this point our great philosophical champion of subjectivity leans heavily in the orthodox direction. At all events Christianity as apprehended and interpreted in the subjectivity of the Hegelian philosopher is little to his taste. The trouble with such doctrines is that Christianity is received and interpreted entirely within the context of some particular philosophy, so that the truth of the interpretation becomes a mere consequence of the speculative truth of the philosophy that does the interpreting. Thus we may notice in some contemporary writers that Christianity has, in fact, made very little difference to their general philosophical views, and that indeed the case for these philosophical views would be just as strong or as weak as it is now if we dismissed Christianity from the picture altogether.

For example, as expressed in the writings of Paul Tillich, the Tillichian philosophy is highly integrated with that conception of Christianity which the Tillichian philosophy encourages and fosters. Nevertheless, the case for the Tillichian philosophy would not in the least be weakened if all the references to Christianity were eliminated from the Tillichian writings. In other words, Dr. Tillich indicates that, given a certain interpretation of Christianity, Christianity is compatible with the

Tillichian philosophy. But certainly the Tillichian philosophy no more requires Christianity than Christianity requires the Tillichian philosophy. Their cohabitation in his writings remains essentially accidental. Similarly with the influence of Heidegger on Bultmann. Bultmann can show that, given a certain interpretation of it, Christianity is compatible with Heidegger and existentialism, but he can hardly claim that either requires the other, and certainly the case for Heidegger is neither strengthened nor weakened by its alliance with Christianity in Bultmann's writings.

The type of Christian apologetic so savagely assailed by Kierkegaard was, of course, predominantly Hegelian in its philosophical outlook. Contemporary apologetics, a century or so later, is no longer frankly Hegelian, although in a subtle way nineteenth-century idealism is still perhaps more influential than is usually apparent or admitted. We may truly say, however, that the phenomenon observed by Kierkegaard is an apologetic theology characterized by a certain conception of the nature and purpose of apologetics, and by a methodology of apologetics, which still dominates the mind of the so-called and self-called liberal theologian.

Of course every Christian thinker requires some overruling conception of his office and function. Clearly his task is that of communication. The Christian content must not merely be expressed, but so expressed that others may find it both intelligible and cogent. As a bare statement of the purpose of the apologist this is unlikely to meet with any opposition from any Christian quarter whatsoever, but it is always possible to combine this definition of the function of an apologist with so narrow a conception of his methodology that his task becomes in effect not that of communicating Christianity but rather that of reconceiving Christianity in a form that is communicable by a particular strategy of communication. Thus, as so often in twentieth-century educational theory, method triumphs over content. The educator is so obsessed by a particular strategy of communication that what cannot be expressed in his par-

ticular way ceases to be either capable or worthy of expression.
Similarly the apologist finds that in order to communicate
Christianity in his particular way he must first of all rewrite
and reconceive it.

Thus for the kind of apologist we are discussing, the conception of the method is prior to the conception of the function.
The aim becomes one of intruding Christianity into a point of
view that Christianity itself has done nothing to form. Instead
of saying, in effect, to the modern man, "If you will adopt a
totally Christian point of view, you will find, perhaps to your
surprise, that things to which you already attribute value and
validity can indeed be gathered up and recognized within the
terms of a Biblical and Christian philosophy of life," the apologist now says, "Without in any way altering or modifying your
previous point of view and philosophy of life you may be led
to rediscover that, with suitable and sufficient qualifications,
Christianity is one of the things that your present point of view
can be stretched to include." In other words the aim of the
apologist is to add Christianity to the secular man's present
list of affirmations, to supplement his existing way of life with
a kind of distilled essence of Christianity, which would enrich but not modify his accustomed systems of thought and
affirmation. Thus the strategy of the apologist is not to change
the characteristically modern convictions and intellectual prejudices, but rather so to modify Christianity that it can be
assimilated to them without making any real difference to
them. The method is one that evades intellectual conflict by
judicious redefinition. "All this," the modern apologist says to
the modern man, "but heaven too; the day of the Lord without the dark night of the soul!"

The theological counterpart of this philosophical conception
of his methodology is usually a frank reductionism. The most
obvious areas in which this occurs in the so-called liberal apologetic theology are those occupied in Christianity by the doctrines of the incarnation and the Trinity. Oddly enough for
thinkers who so stress their modernity these effects are secured

by a return to ancient and outmoded heresies that the Christian
elite rejected, after very full and protracted critical discussion,
centuries ago. Thus, for example, in Christology the general
tendency is to return, by way, of course, of some twentieth-
century-sounding formulation, to a doctrine of the incarnation
that closely resembles the ancient Nestorian heresy. In effect,
this reduces the figure of the Christ to the outstanding example
of the process by which a human being is inspired and guided
through a life of intimacy with and obedience to the immanent
spirit of God. From this point of view the Christ is not unlike
the Christian, or for that matter the non-Christian, saints. We
see accomplished in him absolutely what we see accomplished
in the others more partially and relatively. Sometimes reversion
to primitive heresy is even accompanied by a more or less
learned attempt at a historical demonstration that in fact something very like the Nestorian heresy is identical with the orthodoxy that finally emerged out of the decisions of the Coun-
cil of Chalcedon.

Similarly the modern liberal theologian's treatment of the
doctrine of the Trinity is in effect a return to the modalistic
heresies of the early church, a substantial unitarianism, slightly
modified and compromised in order to make it just barely possible to use the Trinitarian language of the liturgy, at all
events in some poetic and symbolical sense. Again we find this
accompanied by a paradoxical historical argument to the general effect that this is all that orthodoxy ever really meant, even
that this in fact was the doctrine of classical theologians like
Augustine and Aquinas!

But the general spirit of reductionism in apologetic theology
cannot be confined to these two extremely important theological areas. There is a constant tendency to reduce the claims
of spirituality upon life, to minimize the element of the supernatural in Christianity, and in general at all costs to placate
the intellectual tendencies of the time, whether naturalistic or
existentialist, or even both at the same time.

It would seem obvious, if this reductionist strategy of com-

munication is in the modern world the only mode of communication that can possibly communicate anything, that classical,
Biblical Christianity, the authentic Christianity of catholic or
evangelical orthodoxy, cannot be communicated, so that from
this point of view the primary task of the apologist is to reconceive Christianity in what, from the standpoint of this particular technique of communication, is its only possible communicable form. The reaction of the church at large against
what the great mass of Christians cannot but regard as a gross
misrepresentation of everything they stand for is understandable enough, yet not necessarily cogent or well conceived, for
it usually takes the form of a theological scrutiny of liberal
apologetics which demonstrates that this improvised contemporary Christianity is not the real Christianity of the ages at
all. Such a demonstration can easily be carried out, for, after
all, what it demonstrates is the obvious; and the liberal theologian can always reply that, after all, the real trouble is that
from the beginning until now the great majority of Christians
in the church have grossly misunderstood and misinterpreted
Christianity. All the Christian times, apparently, were out of
joint until at last the modern liberal theologians were born to
set them right.

What is really required is a philosophical rather than a historical and theological critique of these liberal positions. It is
to modern error rather than to modern truth that the liberals
have assimilated their Christianity. The trouble with their
methodology has been its uncritical, nonprophetic character.
Its attitude toward modern culture and the forms of its intellectualism have been too sycophantic, which is another way
of insisting that the main office of apologetic is criticism, not
artful assimilation. The apologist fulfills his task by convicting
the contemporary intellectual climate of opinion of philosophical error, and in particular of that kind of philosophical error
that betrays modern man into theological error by persuading
him to affirm faulty metaphysical and epistemological propositions that are logically incompatible with the Christian affirma-

tions. But note that the important thing for the apologists to demonstrate is not that the prevalent and fashionable philosophical positions are incompatible with Christianity — which is usually obvious enough — but rather that they are philosophically in error, so that no honest man should affirm them whether he is a Christian or not.

Of course it must always be true that the apologist should advance from such a critique of contemporary ideas and prejudices to a further critique of the forms of society and social institutions which coexist with, and are to some extent in harmony with, these defective but fashionable ideologies. In other words, I would assimilate the office of the Christian apologist not only to that of the critical philosopher but also to that of the socially critical prophet. In our world it is not only ideas but also prevalent social institutions and prejudices that hold men back from the fullness of Christian faith. True apologetics is a critique of the whole culture rather than merely a critique of its fashionable ideas, indeed, the critique of the ideas is merely one significant aspect of this total critique of the culture.

What we have called liberal theology, because that is what it usually calls itself, is too uncritical of contemporary culture. This may seem a surprising verdict because in many quarters it is usually supposed that liberal theological views are apt to coincide with radical social and political convictions. But the kind of social and political radicalism that often accompanies liberal theology is usually not really radical at all. There is a kind of conservatism that attaches itself to the actual structures and forms of society as they are now — or more often as they were the day before yesterday. But there is another kind of conservatism that attaches itself not to society as it is now, but to the main lines of development characteristic of its present condition.

We may distinguish between a static conservatism that is satisfied with present actualities and a more dynamic kind of conservatism that is satisfied with existing tendencies. The

former would say society as it is now is what it should be — no
doubt with minor modifications — whereas the latter would say
that society as it is now is at least progressing in the direction
in which it ought to progress, and that we need ask no more
than that it should move along these lines of development
more certainly and rapidly. The second of these two points of
view is often described as radical, but it has very little claim to
such a dignified and august title. The true radicalism would be
more likely to say that social development has been moving
along defective lines and shows very little sign of proceeding
in any better direction. It is not merely the present actuality
that is fallen but also its characteristic lines of development. It
is not merely that man is fallen below the level of his nature
now, but also that he is consequently out of line with his des-
tiny. For a truly Christian radicalism the Fall is not only the
Fall of the past and the present, it is also the Fall of the future.
The idea of a radically defective world progressing toward
some future perfection was always a somewhat paradoxical
one, for if it were really so defective as now appears, how
could its characteristic lines of development possibly be so
beneficent? The question of what and where we are is not irrelevant to the question of whither we are tending. The present
indeed is always that which in fact determines the future, so
that a truly radical social criticism must necessarily be a critique of our tendencies and potentialities as well as an attack
on our actualities.

We conclude from this phase of the discussion that the failure of the so-called and self-called liberal theology is not so
much a theological failure as a philosophical one, and that the
philosophical failure is simply one aspect of a vaster prophetic
failure that is fatal to the integrity of Biblical Christianity.

But if the apologist of the type we are criticizing errs by
misconceiving his relationship with contemporary culture, he
errs perhaps even more profoundly by misconceiving his relationship to theology itself. The general tendency of liberal
apologists is to regard their function as one that is best ful-

filled by composing a new theology, but in this they fail to discern the important difference between apologetics and theology. It is certainly the function of the apologist to defend the theologian, to champion his method and his claim to intellectual integrity, even to communicate to the nontheological mind the substance of the theologian's conclusions and their effectiveness as hypotheses that truly succeed in co-ordinating and making sense of the theological data, but it is not the function of the apologist as such to compose and commend a new theology, merely on the grounds that this new theology lends itself to and facilitates his own apologetic procedures.

Of course, there is a sense in which the theologian belongs to the church while the apologist belongs to the world. The theologian is concerned with the problems and questions that the proclamation of the Christian gospel raises in the mind of the believer. Christian faith indeed raises many more questions than at first it answers. Hence its extraordinary power and effectiveness as an intellectual stimulus. The man who recites the Apostles' Creed *ex animo* has many more problems to exercise and evoke the powers of his mind than the man who resolutely declines to do anything of the kind. The apologist, on the other hand, is concerned with the questions that the proclamation of the Christian gospel arouses in the mind of an as yet unbelieving world. These tend to be, of course, very different questions, and upon the whole they are far less profound and stimulating. For the same reason the discussion of, shall we say, the problems of nuclear physics among physicists tends to be far more profound and searching than a similar type of discussion carried on by interested nonphysicists. Apologetics is an ecclesiastical activity that takes place on the frontiers of Christian commitment. Its discussions are necessarily of a somewhat elementary character, and many of the deepest and profoundest problems of theology never arise at all.

The secular analogy to contemporary apologetics is that attempt to communicate to a nonscientifically trained audience the essentials of the scientific outlook, and of the conclusions to which the scientific method has led those who have devotedly employed it. These popular books, which seek to communicate the essential drift of events in the sciences to the nonscientific world, have often had brilliant success and have sometimes been superbly well written, but we should all agree that it is not the function of such a scientific apologist to compose new scientific theories on the ground that he finds them easier to communicate than the actual ones. Science itself is inevitably prior to the scientific apologetic, just as Christian theology itself is prior to Christian apologetics. The apologist's job is thus to communicate to the nonspecialist the conclusions of the specialized theologians, and to explain the methods by which they have achieved them, and all this in language and concepts familiar or readily available to those to whom he addresses himself.

In general we may say that the sole purpose of theology is to get at, to grasp, and to articulate more and more faithfully, the essential content, implications, and presuppositions of the gospel. The theologian aims only at truth. It is a great mistake to suppose that there can be other kinds of theology built up round distinct purposes. Thus we must protest against any notion of a special ecumenical theology, a kind of theological ideology formulated for the express purpose of facilitating the reunion movement. If genuine Christian theology does not provide a solid basis for the movement toward a Christian reunion, it is useless to formulate a so-called " ecumenical " theology for that special purpose. Similar exception may be taken to phrases like " a social theology " or, " the social gospel." Again, if genuine theology does not imply or impose a prophetic critique of our existing and fallen social orders, it is useless to embark upon the composition of a special social theology in order to fulfill that purpose. The same stricture would apply to any attempt to compose a special apologetic theology. Once more, if real theology is not a science and a teaching that is for and addressed to mankind as such, it is useless to improvise some popular substitute that, as can very easily be detected, turns out to be no genuine Christian theology at all but a mere baseless syncretism of selected Biblical ideas fused together with notions derived from idealist philosophy and ethics, vitalistic interpretations of evolution, and the like.

For one thing it soon becomes obvious to the observer, even to the observer whose acquaintance with Christianity and the Christian church is slight, that the apologetic theology which is being supplied to him is not real theology at all. This is one of the reasons why so many of the Christian elites, who compose these apologetic theologies, feel so estranged from the mass of their fellow Christians, and from the kind of teaching and evangelism that spiritually sustains them. For one of the causes of the prevalent nonacceptance of the liberal apologetic theology by the great mass of non-Christians is their observation that this theology is perhaps even more overwhelmingly rejected by the great mass of Christians. One reason why the theological liberal cannot convert the world is his very obvious failure to convert the church. It is this spectacle which gives the worldling, to whom the apologetic is addressed, his suspicion of the intellectual integrity of the apologist, his misgiving that the apologist is affixing the Christian label to something to which no real Christian would ever dream of attaching it.

For the obvious fact is that the overwhelming majority of the Christian masses, and even a by no means negligible proportion of the Christian elites, are not convinced by what we have called the liberal apologists. I remember years ago in England the sensation aroused when a bishop, anything but a rigidly orthodox Anglo-Catholic one, remarked that it was impossible to run a parish along the lines indicated by the Modern Churchmen's Union. He also condemned at the same time the use of the poetically and musically elite, but theologically somewhat reductionist, hymnal *Songs of Praise*. There can be little doubt, I think, that there was a great deal of truth in his strictures. Somehow or other the liberal apologetic presentation of Christianity does not stimulate the laity to heroic spirituality

and santification, nor does it move the ministry to really profound and dedicated pastoral labors. If we are to use any kind
of pragmatic test — "Ye shall know them by their fruits" — we
shall unhesitatingly be compelled to observe the superiority of
what we may describe as the more orthodox modes of Christian proclamation and expression. No doubt this will not move
the orthodox very much, for they have never been impressed
by pragmatic and instrumentalist types of philosophy, but it
should at all events have its sting for those theological liberals
who have gone in for them rather enthusiastically.

No doubt one of the reasons for the comparative ineffective-
ness of liberal apologetic theologies is their pronounced class
basis. On the whole it is true to say that this kind of theology
has historically been of and for the middle classes, or at all
events of and for the refined and cultivated members of the
middle classes. It is perhaps for this reason that this kind of
theology has had rather more success in America than elsewhere, for the United States has become the great middle-class
society, related to the middle classes of the world rather as
Russia is related to the proletarians of the world. In the nineteenth century religious liberalism was particularly related to
idealist philosophy in general and especially, of course, to
Hegel. In the twentieth century it is still recognizably in the
same succession, with various brands of pragmatism and existentialism substituted for Hegel, but the constituency more
or less unchanged.

Of course the middle classes themselves have changed their
character in the meantime. The economic basis of the older
middle classes was the ownership of property, whereas that of
the newer middle classes, who have in many cases recently
emerged from the proletariat by meritoriously climbing the
modern educational ladder, is now the possession of technical
and managerial skills and the enjoyment of relatively high in-
comes. Nevertheless the new middle classes, although by no
means identical with the older middle classes, still aim to be
and to remain as their legitimate sociological successors, shed-

ding perhaps the puritanism but still pretending to a rather watered-down version of the "gracious living" and gentility.

It is to these classes that the liberal apologist most easily speaks, perhaps because it is from these classes that most usually he has himself emerged. But the great mass of Christian people, of course, are drawn from many other social groups besides the middle classes, and an expert understanding of their special needs and affinities is of little use so far as the great mass of mankind is concerned. We have already observed, for example, the preoccupation of so much of the contemporary apologetic with existentialism and psychiatry, so that in America in particular the liberal pastoral ministry often becomes little more than a specialized and religious form and application of psychiatry, a particular way of wrestling with the psychological pressures and problems characteristic of the middle classes in our society. Yet it still remains true, even in the West, even in America, that the great mass of people are for the most part in an overly extroverted technical mood, more interested in nature and natural science than in human frailties, obsessed by science fiction and tangible purposes, intellectually speaking, more open to the cosmological argument or the five ways of Thomas Aquinas than to existentialist German theology, to Heidegger, Bultmann, or Tillich. In fact, the world that seems ready for and responsive to this particular approach is a minority world, the world of the refined and worried middle classes.

But even in saying this we forget that no doubt the majority in this middle-class world itself is neither overly refined nor excessively anxious, and that, after all, a sociological analysis of human beings into component classes and groups, each with its general tendencies and characteristics, must never be pushed so far as to lead us to forget that, after all, men are everywhere men. We must never blind ourselves to the underlying, often heavily disguised, but nevertheless in the long run massively effective, universal human nature. Many modern thinkers distrust the concept of this massively effective human nature, perhaps because they suppose that it is some kind of Platonic universal. It is, of course, always possible that it is indeed just that, and none the worse on that account. And there is nothing particularly modern about distrusting the Platonic universal. This distrust was characteristic of the nominalism that dominated the later Middle Ages, and the Christian theologian in particular has the best of all possible reasons, based on his disillusioning experience, for distrusting that distrust. What remains of the Christian doctrine of the incarnation, that God in Jesus Christ became man, if we have so diminished in value and significance the term "man" that it now means little more than merely "one of the men," so that, to use modern existentialist language, Jesus now shares with us not our nature — from this point of view there is none to share — but our condition; even perhaps — to complete the sorry story of the reduction of the concept of the incarnation to futility and vanity by the liberal theologians — our sinful condition? At all events, it is worth reminding ourselves that human beings belong to the human race more profoundly than they belong to the middle or any other class, and that to address them at the deepest level is always to address man as such.

Thus perhaps the great failure of the middle classes in the world of the nineteenth and the twentieth centuries is the failure to confront the proletarian mind, whether we find it inside or outside the church, the failure, for example, to cope with the challenge of Marxism, which in many ways has more in common with Christian orthodoxy than with Christian liberalism. For Marxism also believes in objective truth, and is suspicious of existentialist and psychiatric approaches to the problem of man, whereas Christian orthodoxy also takes the creation and effectiveness of matter seriously, and sees in God's dialectical mastery and disposition of the material world one of the means in and through which he effects and affirms his lordship over all history.

In other words, as we face the condition of the world as it now is we begin to question even the timeliness of the liberal apologetic theology, above all, the characteristic on which it has prided and plumed itself. In so far as it has shown itself relatively effective in its dealings with modern men, it has confined itself to the most literate and responsive of them. It has produced a sophisticated theology for the sophisticates, and has never even troubled to consider either the great problem of the mass man or, still less, the very real virtues of mass thought. At its worst it becomes an academic theology for the academics, and particularly those academics busily at work at the study of literature and the humanities, those most of all impressed with the reality of symbolism and the profound existential experience of the characters caught up in the subtleties of classic and modern drama. To the scientist and technician the liberal apologetic theologies are far less acceptable, and to the great mass of professing and practicing Christians least acceptable of all.

But in describing what we have called the liberal apologetic theology as primarily a sophisticated theology by and for the academics we have not, perhaps, even then indicated its primary and especial milieu. This kind of theology has traditionally been most of all at home in seminaries and places of theological learning. Its appeal is particularly to men preparing for the ministry of the church who have become somewhat doubtful of the validity of their faith and the meaning of their vocation, and, in many cases, are passing through a mildly neurotic phase brought about by the anxieties that their doubt precipitates. Thus, perhaps, the chief target and most important recipient of this kind of apologetic ministry is not so much the man outside the faith but the man inside the faith who is beginning to falter where before he so firmly trod.

Of course, theological students, like the men preparing for any other of the so-called learned professions, are by no means all of equal or first-class ability. I recollect hearing a professor of medicine discoursing on the general theme that it was a great mistake to suppose that all medical students should be men of first-class mental caliber. In the first place, he argued, the number of men available of this quality is bound to be small and other professions besides medicine will undoubtedly take their quota. In any case there is no reason why the man of more moderate ability should not become a faithful and effective medical practitioner. His conclusion was that it was neither necessary nor possible, nor perhaps even desirable, that only men with the very highest intelligence quotients should enter the medical schools.

The same thing is, of course, true also of the theological schools. Seminaries certainly do succeed in getting their fair share, perhaps slightly more than their fair share, of really gifted and brilliant students, but, of course, like law, medicine, and other professions they have to take in many others also, well knowing that a fine and fruitful ministry can come from men who could not possibly be described as intellectually brilliant. As things are in our culture today it is perhaps especially among the brighter mediocrities — men with sufficient ability to appreciate the strength of what the world says in criticism of the faith, yet of insufficient critical power to discern its weaknesses — that very real intellectual difficulties and doubts occur, and it is perhaps particularly to such men that the liberal apologetic theology, with its reservations and reductionism, has a genuine appeal; perhaps, in tiding them through a difficult period, it performs a real service. We may even characterize this kind of theology as a special theology of the seminary and for the faltering seminarian. Thus, considered as a phase of man's intellectual and spiritual growth, as a stage in development through which many men need to pass, we may be able to achieve a sympathetic understanding of it. The danger, of course, is that growth may be retarded at this particular phase and the student pass out of the seminary with a theology of and for the seminary community that may very well be worse than useless in and to the parish to which he goes. Woe betide him indeed if he spends the rest of his life talking to his parishioners as though they were potential seminarians who never quite made the grade.

Of course, it is my own conviction that what is usually called orthodoxy in Christian theology is superior to liberal apologetic theology primarily as scientific theology. But although I would lay less stress upon it, of this also I am equally convinced, that theological orthodoxy is far more closely in touch with the mind of the mass of mankind and with the kind of perennial philosophy that articulates and enriches the virtue of that mind; is far more communicable to men as such everywhere than the elite, liberal apologetic theology which speaks today out of, rather than to, the middle-class refinement of our own age, in its present form almost certainly doomed to pass away rapidly.

Chapter VII

The Perennial Philosophy

The theme of this final chapter is perhaps not an unfamiliar one. It will certainly not come as a surprise to the diligent reader who has borne so far with this book. The proper language and thought world of the theologian, the form of experience out of which and with respect to which he must speak, and in the long run the authentic mode of communication both to the elites and to the masses, is that which is provided by what has been called "the perennial philosophy," or sometimes, more poetically, "the refreshing stream." I am aware, however, that the phrase "the perennial philosophy" is an extremely ambiguous one, so that our main task here will be to characterize it more clearly and precisely. We may perhaps proceed by considering in turn four important questions: (1) What is the perennial philosophy? (2) Where is the perennial philosophy? (3) What are the chief points of contrast between the perennial philosophy and the various antagonistic schools of philosophy in the modern Western world? (4) What is the theological relevance of this *philosophia perennis?*

What Is the Perennial Philosophy?

Like all forms of philosophy that are systematically thought out and critically defended, the perennial philosophy is an elite activity. Yet at the same time the perennial philosophy is unsophisticated — or nonsophisticated — in the Platonic sense. It is continuous with the forms of mass experience and mass thought. In aim, at least, it is as broad and comprehensive as the ordinary unsophisticated man's apprehension of life in its concreteness and totality. It is not the task of the perennial philosopher to oppose one aspect of experience to another, or to reduce the scale and richness of the human apprehension of life. We may describe it as the mass experience expressed, articulated, and interpreted by elite thought in elite language.

In this sense it is above all the democratic philosophy, not necessarily because it defines and expounds democracy, but because it responds to democracy's deepest needs and formulates its prevailing intellectual values. It discerns and defines the true wisdom of the masses. Above all, it values and covets for the elites the supreme values of mass thought, its openness to the variety of experience, and its constant orientation toward the total and the concrete. The philosophical consequence of this is a yearning to do justice to every significant element in the experience of men, its abhorrence of any tendency toward easing the task of the philosopher by simplifying his vision of his complex datum.

In consequence it has a nonselective attitude toward the vast accumulation of possible philosophical premises and points of departure which the richness of human experience indicates. What is the use, it would ask, of a philosophy that seems to be quite a good philosophy of this or that, but is for that very reason a poor philosophy of anything else? What is the use, for example, of a well-articulated, plausible, and impressive philosophy of nature and natural science if it is at the same time a poor philosophy of history; and, perhaps, considered as a philosophical interpretation of human experience (or, to use the fashionable phrase, as an existentialism) it is little more than a nonstarter? Conversely, what is the value of a heady, intoxicating existentialism if it is absolutely useless as a philosophy of nature? Or again, what is the use of an epistemology that has nothing to say ontologically, a theory of knowledge that cannot grasp the possibility of any knowledge of being, or think in terms of the being of knowledge? Or what, on the other hand, is the value of a system of ontology that has no epistemological relevance or consequences?

Human existence is an almost infinitely complex thing, in nature, in society, in history, for itself, and for and before God, the infinite and eternal other. Yet, as I have said, in the concrete reality these various aspects and dimensions of human existence are not detachable from one another. Man is not merely in nature and in history at the same time; both nature and history are present and recapitulated in him. Nor is existential man detachable from natural and historical man; rather, the natural and historical man is the existential man. Nor, again, is man for himself distinct from the man who is for and before God. The only valid philosophy, one that is as concrete and all-embracing as life itself, must necessarily be a philosophy that functions at the same time as a successful philosophy of nature and natural science, as a valid philosophy of art, as a profound and prophetic philosophy of history, as an authentic existentialism, as a genuine philosophy of religion, and as a faithful interpretation of Christianity — all at the same time. Only thus can it fulfill its objective to see life steadily and whole.

To describe the perennial philosophy in these terms is, of course, to describe its aims and its purposes rather than its achivements. But at least it is true that, once we are possessed and imbued by such a vision of the purpose and function of philosophy, we shall not rest content with any philosophy that contents itself with some smaller and inferior objective. The subject matter of philosophy is identical with the content of experience — everything. For experience as a philosophical concept denotes not merely the vast collection of the things that have been experienced already, but also the experiences that are potential rather than actual, the experiences that are yet to be. In other words, genuine experience opens the mind to the possibility of further experience; it does not close the mind in some unphilosophical obsession with the experiences that merely are. Actual experience is presumably finite; but conceptual, philosophical experience is infinite.

Where Is the Perennial Philosophy?

But, it may well be said, the aims and ideals of the perennial philosophy may perhaps be more easily described and defined than located in actual philosophical history. Undoubtedly the notion of a *philosophia perennis* in modern philosophical discussion has emerged out of the great return to medieval studies in general and to Thomistic philosophy in particular, which has been so characteristic of Roman Catholic intellectualism since Pope Leo XIII issued his encyclical *Aeterni Patris* in 1879. The study of the history of Western philosophy, and the theological renaissance of the Roman Church is greatly indebted to this immensely significant initiative. At its feeblest, perhaps, modern Neo-Scholasticism is simply a textbook Thomism which is content to quote Aquinas as though he were some final court of philosophical appeal. At its best, however, what has gradually emerged out of this revival and tends more and more to prevail is a new understanding of the breadth and inclusiveness of the medieval mood and achievement in philosophy. At the same time the medieval scholars have increasingly merged with and reinforced those classical scholars who have brought about a rediscovery and new interpretation of the greatness of ancient Greek philosophy. Out of this movement has come a new ability to criticize constructively and to appreciate the characteristic weaknesses of modern philosophy.

It is important, however, that this rediscovery of the greatness and strength of ancient and medieval philosophy, and the use of the insights it brings with it in a critical handling of the history of modern philosophy, should not be interpreted as a merely reactionary movement. It would be crass foolishness to suppose that the authority and power of ancient and medieval philosophy can be reinstated in modern philosophical debate by the magisterial quotation of ancient and medieval philosophers. We shall defer this particular aspect of the discussion to the next section of this chapter.

It is the movement, despite the greatness and lucidity of

Aquinas, from Thomism in particular to medievalism in general, that makes it possible for us to appreciate the massive continuity between ancient Greek and medieval Christian philosophy. Just as the two dominating names in the record of ancient Greek philosophy are Plato and Aristotle, so in the story of medieval philosophy the two greatest names are Augustine and Thomas — Augustine, the Christian Platonist, and Thomas, the Christian Aristotelian. Just as the differences between Plato and Aristotle are very real and must be carefully appreciated but can nevertheless be easily exaggerated, so it is also with Augustine and Thomas. They differ significantly and yet at the same time they magnificently converge. Even within the Middle Ages Thomas did not prevail over Augustine. Most of the great medieval philosophers, for example, Anselm and Bonaventura, were Augustinians, and we do not find any truly great Thomists among the successors of Thomas until we come to the threshold of the modern period. On the whole we must say that throughout the Middle Ages the Augustinian mode of thought prevailed, and that through many channels it had the more decisive influence upon the modern world. Thus the Protestant Reformers were enormously influenced by Augustine — although rather more, it must be confessed, by his pessimistic anthropology than by his Platonic rationalism. In some ways more decisive perhaps was the movement of the new physics away from Aristotle toward a more Platonic type of formulation which, as we have seen, still holds the center of the stage to this day.

It is a strange paradox that although Aristotle was much more interested than Plato in what we should nowadays call scientific questions, it was in fact Platonism, filtering down to the modern world through Augustine and the Augustinians, which supplied the early modern scientists with their philosophical outlook, and Platonism, in this general sense, which has been more heavily reinforced by the achievements of modern science, particularly in physics but also elsewhere, than any other mode of philosophizing. Of Platonism we can truly say that it is more a mode of philosophizing than a particular brand of philosophical doctrine. Indeed, we do not know with any certainty precisely what it was that Plato thought and taught, but we have a very clear apprehension of the way in which he set about the intellectual task.

The outmoding of the Aristotelian physics led, perhaps rather unfairly, to a debunking of the authority of Aristotle all along the line. It has been said by some historians of thought that if it had been biology that had made the grade in the early centuries of modern science rather than physics, Aristotle's reputation would not have suffered as it did; for by modern standards his biology is much more acceptable than his physics. The point of this phase of our discussion is that if we are going to locate the *philosophia perennis* in both the Platonic and the Aristotelian streams, then the *philosophia perennis* is something that makes room within its unity for significant differences of philosophical opinion and profound and important philosophical discussions and controversies. In other words, the *philosophia perennis* is not *a* philosophy in the sense in which Hegelianism, for example, is *a* philosophy. Rather, it is a way of philosophizing, informed and inspired by certain common convictions as to the purpose and function of philosophy and the vocation of the philosopher, but not necessarily imposing any particular philosophical proposition.

Of course, if there is a continuity between medieval and ancient Greek philosophy, there is also a very profound discontinuity. Medieval philosophy is Christian — or, in the case of the great Arab philosophers, Moslem — whereas classical Greek philosophy is untouched by the tremendous influences let loose in Hebrew religion. Thus medieval philosophy is Greek philosophy forced open and exposed to influences external to itself, to its own ultimate health and, indeed, its salvation.

I am aware that many Protestant Christians will feel that this particular intellectual development is too Catholic and external to their own history, but such is not in fact the case. Moving in the wake of the Reformers were very important and significant movements of seventeenth-century Protestant Scholasticism. Indeed the *philosophia perennis* is as near Luther as Melanchthon, and perhaps as near to Calvin at times as Calvin himself. To think of the Reformation and the Renaissance as primarily a rejection of medievalism and the *philosophia perennis* in the great form that it takes in the mightiest medieval philosophers is a historical error. Just as by the time Christianity broke into the ancient world, Plato and Aristotle were little more than memories, and vastly inferior forms of classical philosophy were dominant in the intellectual world, so by the sixteenth century the great figures of the high Middle Ages had become, except perhaps here and there, little more than revered names, and nominalism had enjoyed at least two centuries of almost undisputed supremacy.

Thus the medievalism satirized in Erasmus' *Praise of Folly* and in several other Renaissance texts was not the great medievalism of Thomas, Bonaventura, Grosseteste, and Duns Scotus but the endless, subtle logical discussions characteristic of the nominalists and resembling in some ways the twentieth-century contributions of the logical positivists and their successors, the linguistic analysts. It was philosophy petering out in a monotonous diet of indigestible logistics. Orthodox Protestantism — by which I mean not the so-called neo-orthodoxy but the actual theology of the great Reformers — is as continuous with and as congenial to the mood of the *philosophia perennis* as orthodox Catholicism.

Thus we may locate the *philosophia perennis* particularly in classical Greek philosophy and in its continuation in the medieval world, understanding that in the sense of a particular philosophy there is no *philosophia perennis;* interpreting it, rather, as a tradition of realistic and concrete philosophizing which is continuous with, and the articulation of, the experience of the great mass of mankind. In particular it covets and respects the openness of the latter to the immense variety of experience. It thus provides not merely what we may call the natural language of communication but also the elaborate system of flexible concepts in terms of which it is possible for communication between the elite mind and the mass mind to take place.

It is perhaps important for the Christian mind to interpret the development and first magnificent flourishing of this kind of philosophy in ancient Greece, particularly in Plato and Aristotle, in terms of divine providence. If the Hebrew experience developed a language and forms of communication in which the gospel could first of all be given and proclaimed, it was the Greek experience that developed a language and forms of communication in terms of which that gospel could be understood. It is characteristic of Hebrew speech that it affirms simply what it affirms. It is characteristic, however, of the definitive Greek speech that it affirms what it affirms in such a fashion as to indicate at the same time not only the content of the affirmation but also something of the breadth and the extent of its presuppositions and implications. Of course it can be said that this is a characteristic not so much of the language as of the type of mind that employs the language. On the other hand, we cannot but ask ourselves the question as to how far this particular kind of language has contributed to the development of this particular type of mind. We are left with an unanswerable question, not unlike the familiar, Which came first, the hen or the egg?

Nor must we necessarily think of a return to the *philosophia perennis* as in any sense reactionary. It has been characteristic of modern philosophy, and indeed of late medieval nominalism, that it has taught men to think in ways which do not conform to the great traditions of thought enshrined in the *philosophia perennis*. But these new ways of thinking and conceiving have all been, in one way or another, modes of elite sophistication. The fact is that mass thought, with its intuitive intellectual blindness, still thinks in terms of the *philosophia perennis*, without knowing precisely what it is doing, of course. When the ordinary man becomes a philosopher, but somehow contrives throughout the process to remain an ordinary man, he will be some kind of Platonist or Aristotelian, or, if he is a Christian, some kind of Augustinian or Thomist.

We are greatly mistaken when we suppose that thought forms have universally changed. Thus we are told that modern man no longer believes in a flat earth and in an objective up or down. What we fail to notice is that most of the time, i.e., whenever he is not thinking about geography or astronomy, this is precisely what modern man does believe in and express himself in terms of. What we have to consider is not merely why the notions are mistaken but also why they are nevertheless inevitable. We must distinguish between accidental relativities, which are relative to this man and not to that, and universal relativities, which are relative to all of us. The latter even have a certain philosophical justification, for the inevitable subjective point of view of the self-conscious intellectual being is indeed one of the absolutes of the universe; in its own way — as the Augustinians would teach us — a humble creaturely participation in the absolute world view of God.

It is not enough to say that the inevitable human perspective distorts the truth. For the inevitable perspective is a part of the truth. The total scientific truth is approached, ultimately perhaps even reached — although this is an eschatological dream — not so much by roughly imposing the objective, scientific view on the subjective, human perspective as by approximating the latter to the divine perspective and persuading it to accept its limitations while still comprehending their inevitability. Thus a return to the *philosophia perennis* is not so much a reaction to ancient modes of philosophical thought as a reintegration of elite and mass minds in an intellectual and cultural democracy, precisely that state of affairs into which as yet our political and economic democracy has most tragically failed to grow.

The *Philosophia Perennis* and Modern Philosophy

What modern philosophy chiefly lacks (and to a considerable extent its loss of prestige in our world is due to this defect) is that sense of coherence and chronic continuity which has been one of the most impressive characteristics of the history of modern science. Of course, more closely scrutinized, the story of modern science itself is full of the sudden leaps that occur when the great geniuses who are the heroes of the story arrive at their strange, unlooked-for, and epoch-making hypotheses. Nevertheless these links are within the continuum. Although they strain by suddenly accelerating it, they do not break it.

Of course it is true that we cannot expect the history of philosophy to resemble too closely the history of science. For one thing, great philosophical hypotheses do not go out of date in quite the way that important scientific hypotheses become outmoded. The Ptolomaic astronomy was a splendid achievement of the human intellect, but no one would dream of reviving it. By contrast the central concepts of Platonic philosophy are still very much alive, and no doubt will continue to be so for an indefinite period. I remember some years ago asking a very modern-minded but intelligent student, who was very scornful of Plato and the ancients, to read the account of Socrates' dispute with Thrasymachus in Book II of Plato's *Republic*. To her own surprise she was very much excited by it and saw in it, quite correctly, a thoroughly up-to-date refutation of fascism. Neverthless, if we look at the history of philosophy from, shall we say, the earlier Greek philosophers to Duns Scotus, we cannot but observe something very similar to the massive continuity and integrity of modern scientific development. Ancient and medieval philosophy is the story of genuinely coherent advance, whereas by contrast the story of modern philosophy is one in which the philosophers to a very large degree violently and arrogantly react against one another.

Part of the trouble with modern philosophy is the way in which each new philosophical insight seems to demand the composition of an entirely new philosophy in order to contain it, so that the new insight overthrows rather than enriches the existing conditions of philosophical thought. Contemporary examples of this process are the ways in which the genuine existential insights are gradually frozen into set forms of existentialism. Similarly the insights of a great master like Whitehead congeal into the so-called process philosophy, and those of the logical positivists and linguistic analysts coagulate into a massive, a priori condemnation of all other philosophy whatsoever. There seems to remain no central theme of philosophical development which each new generation and mode of philosophical insight can enrich. There is no cumulative element in the process; almost every philosopher seems to be in a state of more or less frenzied reaction against almost every other. It is as though it were the ambition of every philosopher to give his name to some new brand of philosophy rather than merely to serve in his own humble fashion the cause of philosophy itself. We may say that the mood of modern philosophy has been imperialistic in this sense. Thus our purpose here is not so much to deny the brilliance or detract from the achievement of the great modern philosophers as to quarrel with their ethics.

Another important contrast between the *philosophia perennis* and the prevailing spirit of modern philosophy is the much greater preoccupation with epistemological problems which we find in the period since Descartes. The ancients and the medievals were of course concerned with epistemology, but they saw it much more as an analysis of the act of knowing, a critique of our actual knowledge, rather than as an attempt to answer in somewhat a priori fashion the questions, What kind of thing are we able to know, and to what extent? In particular, epistemology tends in modern philosophy to be regarded as logically prior to any possible ontological scheme. This is perhaps impossible, for any epistemological doctrine will inevitably imply and presuppose some kind of ontological scheme, and perhaps the ancients were right in supposing that it is only in the context of and in terms of some doctrine of man's place in the whole order of reality that epistemological problems can properly be handled. It must be obvious, for example,

that a positivistic doctrine that denies to man any capacity for
metaphysical knowledge, or even of asking metaphysical questions, is one that either takes a rather low view of the place of
human mind in the scheme of reality or holds that the things
which can be the objects of positive knowledge (i.e., perceptual and scientific knowledge) are the only things that exist.
Either of these doctrines is of the ontological and metaphysical
kind, so that, even in this extreme case, what looks like a purely
epistemological doctrine turns out to have some kind of shad-
owy ontological basis.

The notion that epistemology is the first step in philosophy
reached perhaps its highest point in Kant's *Critique of Pure
Reason*. In the course of the last brilliant phase of his career,
Kant gave us his *Critique of Pure Reason,* his *Critique of
Practical Reason,* and (perhaps most brilliant of all) his *Critique of Judgment.* However, what he never got around to giving us was his Critique of the Critiques, and to this day a Critique of the Critical or Epistemological Reason in the Kantian
vein is a task that still has to be undertaken. Certainly this is
not the place to attempt it, but it may in passing be suggested
that a presuppositionless epistemology is impossible, and that
the presuppositions of any epistemology must always and inevitably be ontological. To maintain this point of view would
obviously involve a severe critical judgment upon the mood,
manner, and achievements of modern philosophy as a whole.

A further and perhaps even more serious criticism of modern
philosophy, particularly in its more recent phases, which have
gathered momentum with the professionalization of modern
philosophy (there is now hardly any significant philosopher
who does not hold a university teaching post) is the specialization of philosophers in particular and relatively narrow areas
of philosophical study. Specialization and humble self-confine-
ment to some narrow area of scientific study have become so
essential an aspect of the organizations for scientific research
and teaching that philosophy becomes more and more prone
to imitate it, quite forgetting that philosophy and science are

two very different things. Science is inevitably highly selective
of its subject matter, whereas the whole aim of philosophy is
the contemplation and interpretation of all things whatsoever
in their concrete togetherness. Nowadays there are remarkably
few philosophers in this classical sense. On the contrary, we
have highly specialized professors of logic, ethics, aesthetics,
the philosophy of history, the philosophy of religion, and so
on. The general tendency of such men is to suppose that what
is cogent and plausible in their own relatively narrow sphere
must somehow be shown to be equally cogent and plausible in
every other sphere. They build up a doctrine that is relatively
successful in the interpretation of their own selected set of data
and then apply the same doctrine roughly and ruthlessly to all
other sets of data.

But we may very well hold that this particular way of or-
ganizing philosophical studies and research is foreign to the
very nature of philosophy. If we find a professor of ethics who
makes almost a virtue of knowing nothing in particular about
aesthetics, we may rightly suspect his judgment, even as a professor of ethics. The logician who is indifferent to metaphysics
or the philosophy of religion is in all probability unreliable
even as a logician. For that matter the philosopher of religion
who is indifferent, shall we say, to logic and social philosophy
cannot be trusted even as a philosopher of religion. Philosophy
is concerned with everything in general, and is therefore incompatible with a specialized and exclusive addiction to the
study of anything in particular. All science is rightly abstract
because it abstracts its own particular set of data from all possible contexts and seeks to know and interpret it as it is in and
for itself. Philosophy, however, is inevitably and rightly concerned with the concrete, with the real world in which the
context of anything is everything and ultimately nothing is
totally irrelevant to anything else.

It is true that the term " concrete " is currently much abused
by philosophers and others, particularly existentialists. Again
and again we find the word " concrete " used as the equivalent

of "particular," as the single object of an isolated act of perception. Thus, for example — and here we come to the essence of nominalism — the particular individual man John Smith is held to be concrete, whereas the Platonic universal man is regarded as abstract. The suggestion seems to be that the object of the particular perception is concrete whereas the content of a concept is abstract. To this we must object strongly, for it is the particular percept that is most of all and inevitably abstract. To look at this is necessarily not to look at that, whereas the real world contains both this and that in inescapable relationship to each other. Abstraction, in other words, is not the fruit of conceptual thinking. Abstraction is a process rooted in the limitations of perception, in which we seem to see a large number of things *as though* they existed independently of the many things we do not perceive.

Philosophy from this point of view may be defined as an attempt to overcome the inherent limitations of perception by calling upon the new world of conception to set right its inevitable imbalance. Perception perceives things as though they were separate from and quite independent of one another. Philosophy conceives the imperceptible concrete reality, the togetherness and primordial mutuality of things. Thus we may say in religious terms that man conceives what God perceives; i.e., that the creation is one and yet many at the same time, so that always we are confronted in the world by the one in the many and the many in the one. Theologically speaking, of course, the Trinitarian will say the same thing even of God. Thus we may validly say — paradoxical though this may sound to many people after many centuries of naive and uncriticized nominalism — that perception and science are inevitably abstract in a world of intellectual studies in which philosophy alone seeks the concrete.

From the standpoint of Christian philosophy the only valid abstraction is God. The creation, the entire realm of the not-God, contains no ultimately valid abstraction, for it is impossible to give an altogether adequate and true account of anything in it without reference to the many other things in it, and, above all, without reference to God. But Christian philosophy does conceive of God as entirely independent of the creation and altogether complete in himself. Ultimately, therefore, God is the one valid abstraction, because this is the one case in which the product of the abstraction is at the same time absolutely identical with the concrete reality. All other abstractions, however necessary and however fruitful, contain within themselves a margin of error and an element of inadequacy that we must learn to allow for in all our thinking.

There are, of course, significant and relatively independent areas of philosophical thought, and many of our worst philosophical errors arise because we exaggerate the relative independence into an absolute one. Human experience, because such is the nature of man, may be analyzed into three major areas of contrast. Since most philosophers love dualisms and dichotomies, they usually prefer to analyze and classify on the basis of a twofold scheme. For methodological reasons I prefer always to employ a threefold scheme. If we divide reality into two, nothing remains but the sharpness of the distinction and the inevitable tendency so to accentuate the distinction as to mistake it for an antithesis. Examples are the so-called mind-body problem, the distinction between subject and object, and so on. The habit of making threefold distinctions not only conforms more subtly to the actual order of our experience but delivers us from the dangers of the merely antithetical method in philosophy, as a result of which almost every philosopher finds himself repeatedly impaled on the horns of some other philosopher's dilemma.

The first of these three areas of human experience is that of nature. We have already shown that nature is not merely the primary context of human existence, it is also within human existence itself, for man finds natural processes going on not only around him but also within him. Man recapitulates nature in the very act of transcending it. In knowing nature he intellectually transcends it, but what he knows is something that he finds inevitably present within himself. Thus man both transcends the order of nature and at the same time finds himself immanent within that order. The second vast area of human experience is the sphere which we may indicate by such words as history, society, and culture. Again man transcends this order in the act of knowing and passing judgment upon it, yet at the same time finds the historical, the social, and the cultural as essential ingredients within himself. His relationship to it is again a reflection of the paradox which we find in the divine relationship to the world — both transcendent and immanent. The third area is one that modern philosophy has taught us to term existentialist. It is because man, although he belongs to nature and to history, yet at the same time transcends the natural and the historical or social, that he finds himself involved in the existential, the area of his transcendence.

At this point, of course, the existentialists begin to differ. According to the irreligious existentialists, man in his transcendence of nature and culture, experiencing himself as existing independently of his environment, is man alone for himself. Oddly enough such thinkers conceive of existential man so defined as concrete man, whereas in fact this is abstract man, for man existing independently of his natural and cultural environment is something that we never find in actual experience, something that is indeed unthinkable in actual experience. Merely or exclusively existential man, therefore, as depicted by philosophers of this kind, is not concrete but abstract man. For what we may call the religious existentialists, on the other hand, man in his transcendence of nature and culture is not man alone and for himself but man for and before God, and the man who is for and before God is the concrete man, who not only transcends nature and culture but recapitulates and carries nature and culture within himself.

The philosophical consequences of this threefold structure of human experience are extremely interesting. Clearly an authentic philosophy, one that really corresponds to the aim of the philosopher and responds to his call, is a philosophy that handles the problems of nature, of history-society-culture, and of existence with equal skill; a philosophy that is equally plausible and cogent in all three spheres while nevertheless remaining one philosophy. What, of course, we are often confronted with are philosophies that are born out of an obsession with one of the three areas of experience, are formulated with reference only to the data that confront us in that area, and are then, in a kind of philosophical footnote or afterthought, roughly imposed upon the other two areas with reckless indifference to the extent to which they distort the data confronting us in those areas.

Thus, for example, so long as we have eyes and ears only for the natural area or dimension of human experience philosophies of nature and natural science like naturalism or positivism, or even a Whiteheadian process philosophy, may seem to us plausible enough. The principal reason why naturalism, for example, will not even do as a philosophy of nature is its poor performance as a philosophy of history or existence, for the valid philosophy must be equally efficient in all three spheres. The true datum is not nature in itself but nature considered as the context in which the phenomena and problems of both history and experience have arisen. Nature and natural science are certainly data to which a valid philosophy must do justice, but to do justice to them and nothing else is the bankruptcy of philosophy. Marxism is an example of a philosophy that achieves a certain degree of plausibility and power in the interpretation of history but is rough and crude, considered as a kind of naturalism, and almost worthless, considered as an interpretation of the existential area of human experience. Again, to do some kind of justice to history but insufficient justice to nature and to existence is to fail even as a philosophy of history, for history is not merely itself but that which arises within the context of nature and provides the primary context of existence.

The various brands of existentialism also seem relatively

plausible and cogent so long as we have only existential data in mind. But existentialism fails totally as an interpreter of nature and natural science, a task that it does not usually even attempt — contenting itself with calling it bad names instead. It also fails as a philosophy of history-society-culture because of its ingrained suspicion of the necessary and inevitable collective life, which it tends to regard as a kind of treason against the pure individuality of personal existence. Thus most brands of existentialism are bad even existentially because they misplace and undervalue the extent to which human existence is immanent in its natural and historic contexts and the extent to which it recapitulates them within itself.

Thus, to summarize our three examples: all forms of naturalism fail even as philosophies of nature because they fail as philosophies of history and existence; all forms of historicism, like Marxism, fail even as philosophies of history because they fail as naturalisms and existentialisms; all forms of existentialism fail even as existentialisms because of their inability to interpret history and nature. The valid philosophy must function as a successful naturalism, as an insightful historicism, and as a profound existentialism at one and the same time, and yet in the process remain one integral philosophy.

It is our claim that the *philosophia perennis,* in general at least, always aims at such an ideal as this, and that in the past it has been the Christian versions and variants thereof that have come closest to achieving it. For as we examine the writings of classical Christian theological philosophers such as Augustine, Aquinas, Bonaventura, and Duns Scotus we can see clearly that what they were seeking was precisely a philosophy that would be as comprehensive and concrete as life itself, in precisely the sense which we have had in mind during the last few paragraphs. The form of theology that is closest to the *philosophia perennis,* that breathes, so to speak, the same air and inherits the same ideals and criteria, is what in a very general sense we have termed orthodoxy. The philosophical counterpart of the orthodoxy that triumphed over the ancient heresies is the *philosophia perennis*. The re-emergence of the modern heresies, however, which are identical in substance with the ancient heresies (which they merely rephrase and to some extent reconceive) has been inspired by the various brands of empirically partial and specialized, mutually antithetical, modern philosophies. These philosophies have replaced the *philosophia perennis* in the modern world with such unfortunate consequences.

We are not necessarily arguing at this stage that ancient and medieval philosophers were greater than modern philosophers, or even that their achievement ranks higher. Certainly a list of magnificent philosophical artists such as Plato, Aristotle, Plotinus, Augustine, Aquinas, Bonaventura, and Duns Scotus, though they might perhaps be equaled, could hardly be surpassed, but that sort of comparison is beside the point. Our contention is that ancient and medieval philosophy came closer to the central aims and ideals of philosophy, and more genuinely fulfilled its social and cultural functions, than modern philosophy has succeeded in doing. The student of ancient and medieval philosophy derives a more adequate conception of the purpose of philosophical thought from his studies than the student of modern philosophy, despite the many dialectical brilliances and profound insights that the latter will inevitably encounter.

The Theological Relevance of the *Philosophia Perennis*

Thus breadth and affirmation and a total realism all along the line are the primary characteristics of the *philosophia perennis*. But these, as we saw in an earlier chapter, are characteristic also of the mass mind. The mass mind without brutalization and the elite mind uncorrupted by sophistication meet in the *philosophia perennis*. That is why it has been contended here that the *philosophia perennis,* with the kind of language it has created and sustained, remains the proper and appropriate mode of Christian communication.

In the first place Christian communication requires a total

realism. The doctrine of the creation certainly requires a realistic affirmation and concept of material realities and natural
events. The creation under God really is, and is what it seems
to us to be in our experience of it, whether we experience it
merely by casual and external perception or by scientific meas-
urement and insight. What we must insist upon is that nature
is not a closed system but is continually responsive to the
divine initiative. In other words, we cannot tolerate a naturalism that contrives to be realistic about nature in such a fashion
that it is incapable of being realistic about anything else. The
survival of eighteenth-century deism in the form of a dogmatic
naturalism that makes, for example, miracle impossible is bad
not merely because such concepts inevitably make Christian
affirmation and communication impossible but also because it
is philosophically misconceived and indefensible.

The doctrine that nothing exists except nature and that, in
consequence, nothing exists except that kind of thing which is
appropriately known in the natural sciences is clearly not an
item of knowledge that is known, nor a hypothesis that could
be substantiated, by the methods of the natural sciences. On
the contrary, it is clearly a piece of speculative metaphysics,
which thus can even be rejected as formally self-contradictory.
Of course the naturalistic principle can be so stated that it becomes not an item of philosophical knowledge but a mere rule
of intellectual procedure. In that case, it is only necessary to
say that it is an arbitrary and unnecessary rule, and one by
which we resolutely decline to be bound. In any case, such a
naturalism can hardly function as a philosophy of either history
or existence. We have already bound ourselves to another rule
of intellectual procedure, according to which a philosophy that
is plausible and cogent in one area of human experience but
useless in the interpretation of another must be rejected even
in that area of experience in which it can plausibly function.

This is important for Christian communication, for the proclamation of the gospel demands that we must be just as realistic about history and personal sanctification and salvation as

about nature. To be realistic about history and the real effectiveness of the divine initiative therein, we have again and
again to be realistic about miracle and the supernatural. To be
realistic about sanctification and Christian existence, we have
to be realistic about experiences such as the reception and enjoyment of grace, and indeed about all the various forms of
mystical experience. Of course there is a difference between
being realistic about material and natural events, about historical events, and about spiritual and mystical events. Nevertheless, there is a close analogy between all three, so that it is possible for the mass mind to be equally realistic in all three
spheres of human experience without being conscious of the
subtle analogies and distinctions among these three variant
but kindred modes of realism. It is, however, the *philosophia
perennis* that enables us to be thus equally realistic all along
the line.

Again, Christianity needs and requires a language that is
able to recognize the broad distinctions that confront us in experience without in any way attempting subsequently to reduce one of the terms in which we report our experiences to
another. Thus in immediate experience we are aware of the
difference between physical and mental events; of the distinction between subject and object, and consequently between
subjective and objective; of the contrast between process and
change and thinghood and persistent identity. It must always
be philosophically dangerous, once experience has confronted
us with broad distinctions of this kind, to cast one of the terms
aside and to interpret everything that confronts us in terms of
the other. Thus, for example, in metaphysical materialism the
mental is conceived as merely a very complicated form of the
material, whereas for metaphysical idealism the material is perhaps the lowest and simplest form of the mental. Again, for
some forms of philosophy, the only truth is the objective truth,
and the word " subjective " becomes almost a term of abuse,
whereas for many forms of existentialism all is subjective and
the word " objective " becomes a term of abuse. Similarly, there

are philosophers according to whom reality is nothing but separate things in external relationship to one another. On the
other hand, there are philosophies that protest that there are
no really separate things at all, and that ultimate reality is
seamless.

All these philosophies are subtle and sophisticated simplifications of reality that must be rejected from the very outset.
Our world contains both material and mental realities, so that
neither materialism nor idealism is acceptable. Similarly, in a
world in which there are subjects there must always be objects,
just as in a world in which there are objects there must always
be subjects. It is inconceivable that the one could exist apart
from the other, and we are therefore compelled to be equally
realistic about objectivity and subjectivity and to do equal justice to the validity of both.

Once more, our world is a world of both things and processes, of both change and persistence, and neither is to be explained away in terms of the other. Indeed, without persistence
change is impossible; for without persistence change would
not really be change at all but a mere procession of novelties,
each one following swiftly upon the next, so that we must be
equally realistic both about change and about continuing and
persisting identity beneath change. Again, we must be equally
realistic about both the natural and the supernatural, for the
one is inconceivable apart from the other. Obviously the supernatural is meaningless in a world in which there is no nature
for it to transcend. Similarly, the existence of the order of nature is inexplicable apart from the affirmation of the supernatural, for the order of nature is emphatically not the kind of
reality that carries within itself the ground and explanation of
its own existence. It is not characterized, in other words, by
the aseity of God.

If the order of nature were self-authenticating, the self-explanatory reality, it would be possible to apply something very
like Anselm's ontological argument for the existence of God in
order to vindicate the necessary existence of nature. As far as

I know, nobody has ever attempted such a task, but if we were
to have an ontological argument for the existence of nature —
and philosophical naturalism really implies its possibility — I
imagine that it would be even easier to reject it than it was
to reject Anselm's original essay in ontological demonstration.
Thus we require a philosophy that will permit us to be as realistic about the supernatural as about the natural.

Now once again, as even the foregoing brief summary clearly
indicates, the grounds for accepting and affirming such a philosophy must clearly be philosophical. Yet, nevertheless, once
we have accepted and affirmed it, we find to our joy, and no
doubt even to our surprise, that this is precisely the kind of
philosophy that the evangelists' affirmation of the Christian
gospel requires and presupposes. Once the apologist makes it
his task to state and defend precisely the philosophy and language that honest Christian evangelism inevitably presupposes,
the gap between the apologist and the evangelist, between the
preacher in the pulpit and the parish minister in the confirma-
tion class, on the one hand, and between the theological professor in his study or on the rostrum, on the other, is at last
abolished. It is perhaps because of the important role played
at least by some versions of the *philosophia perennis* in the
thought of the Roman Catholic Church that that communion
is so much less troubled by mutual suspicion and distrust between evangelist and apologist than most of the other Christian
bodies.

We cannot honestly, of course, accept a certain kind of philosophy and mode of philosophizing merely because it happens to facilitate Christian communication. On the contrary,
we must first of all be persuaded that on philosophical grounds
alone it is both satisfying and defensible. Yet in the long run
the *philosophia perennis*, in almost any one of its various forms,
not merely justifies itself philosophically both as a form of
philosophical affirmation and as a source of philosophical criticism; not only does it facilitate and make possible Christian
proclamation and communication; more generally, it is, above

all, the natural and appropriate philosophy of democratic culture. For in its openness to experience and in the way in which
it lends itself to every possible kind of affirmation and realism,
it is, above all, the philosophy that permits and encourages all
the conceivable kinds of profound and valid human interest
to flourish side by side, not merely with mutual tolerance but
even with mutual respect. Thus we are able to see the recovery
of a philosophical point of view that enables us to resolve the
tensions and dissipate the antagonisms that have arisen within
so many parts of Christendom between the apologists and the
evangelists, between the Christian elites and the Christian
masses. This may indeed be the first step toward recovering a
point of view that enables us to bring about a meeting of the
elites and the masses in our general culture. Thus we may pass,
perhaps dialectically, from the antagonisms that press upon
us so harshly (and that by endangering our unity menace our
peace) into the rich and variegated cohesions that our Western culture requires, not only in order to survive but also in
order to fulfill its own vocation and even its own ideal of itself.

Notes

1. I owe this phrase to Prof. Michael Foster's unjustly neglected little book, *Political Philosophies of Plato and Hegel* (Oxford University Press, 1935). See especially pp. 15 ff.

2. This is the position attributed to the Averroists in a sermon delivered before the University of Paris by Thomas Aquinas. Siger himself never makes any such statement, but he closely approaches it; and it is probable that such a doctrine may rightly be attributed to him and to his fellows. It was perhaps prudence rather than sincere and genuine scruple which dissuaded him from making explicit the last logical consequence of his position.

3. Leopold von Ranke, *Werke* (Leipzig, 1874), Vol. xxxiii–xxxiv, p. vii.

4. Prof. James Barr's *The Semantics of Biblical Language* (Oxford University Press, 1961) arrived alas too late to influence this discussion, but I am delighted to read his searching critique of the Hebraic "Biblical theology" school.

5. Thorleif Boman, *Hebrew Thought Compared with Greek*, translated by Jules L. Moreau (The Westminster Press, 1960).

6. Claude Tresmontant, *A Study of Hebrew Thought*, translated by Michael Francis Gibson (Desclee Co., Inc., 1960).

7. It is significant that Ranke, the first great historical "literalist," was also a Hegelian.

8. Basil Willey, *Christianity, Past and Present* (Cambridge University Press, 1952), pp. 147–148.

9. Cf. Richard Hooker, *The Laws of Ecclesiastical Polity*, Book III (xi), "If the knowledge thereof (i.e., salvation) were possible without natural reason, why should none be found capable thereof only men . . . ?"

10. Donald Mackenzie Mackinnon, ed., *Christian Faith and Communist Faith* (The Macmillan Company, London, 1953), p. 249.

11. *King Lear*, Act II, Scene iv.

12. Sören Kierkegaard, *Concluding Unscientific Postscript*, translated by D. F. Swenson and provided with introduction and notes by Walter Lowrie (Princeton University Press, 1941), p. 51.

13. *Ibid.*, p. 200.

CPSIA information can be obtained at www.ICGtesting.com
Printed in the USA
LVOW011103081212

310700LV00003B/578/P